INTENTIONAL MENTORING
MENTEE'S WORBOOK

Dr. Kenneth D. Davis

INTENTIONAL MENTORING WORKBOOK
Copyright © 2022 Kenneth D. Davis
All rights reserved.

No part of this publication may be reproduced, transmitted, or stored in a retrieval system, in any form or by any means electronic, mechanical, photocopying, recording or otherwise, without the prior permission of the author. This book of curriculum is sole subject to the condition that it shall not, by way of trade or otherwise, be lent, re-sold, hired, or otherwise circulated without the auth's prior consent/permission in any form of binding other than that in which is published and without a similar condition including this condition being imposed on subsequent purchaser.

All scriptures quotations, unless otherwise noted, all scriptures are from the 21ST CENTURY KING JAMES VERSION of the Bible. Copyright© 1994 by Deuel Enterprises, Inc. Used by Permission. Scripture taken from the New King James Version®. Copyright © 1982 by Thomas Nelson. Used by permission. All rights reserved.

ISBN: 978-1-957551-05-0

Cover/Interior Design: Bledsoe Publishing Company LLC

Published by: Bledsoe Publishing Company LLC

Printed in the United States of America

TABLE OF CONTENTS

NOTE TO THE READER	i
INTRODUCTION	iii
PILLAR: LIVING	1
Introduction/Living/Getting to Know You	8
Reaching My Goals	27
Developing Meaningful Relationships	45
Legacy/Cultural EYE	52
PILLAR: LOVING	59
Self-Love/Critical Thinking/Boundaries	68
Love Begins in Me	84
The Power of Giving	100
The Community of Love	115
PILLAR: LEARNING	123
Career Vs. Job	131
Social Media and Digital Responsibility	140
Organization is Key	148
Health and Well-being	157
PILLAR: LAUGHING	167
Laugh Therapy	173
Anger Management	182
Overcoming Stress and Anxiety	196
Express Yourself	212
PILLAR: LEADING	225
Leading Social Change	233
Financial Literacy	248
Character Development	263
Lead by Example	280
PILLAR: LEGACY	297
Understanding Legacy	303
Living your Legacy	316
Creating a Legacy	329
A Living Legacy	343
BIBLIOGRAPHY	359
ABOUT THE AUTHOR	361

NOTE TO THE READER

Dear Reader/Mentee,

Intentional Mentoring is a set of lessons that I have created to help you navigate your journey called life. My hope is that every child, young adult, and/or adult can learn, interact with, and experience a mentor-mentee relationship. In the same way that mentors are special people, mentees are their opportunity to share their life lessons and wisdom with. This Mentee's Workbook provides you (the reader/mentee) with invaluable information that will prepare you for the next steps in your life. It made the difference for me, and my hopes are… it will do the same for you!

LIVING life has been a challenge yet I'm LEARNING that LAUGHING and LOVING are free, easy, and provides opportunities that I could have missed. I've grown up in poverty, disadvantaged communities, and have had obstacles to overcome. Haven't we all! Yet if it had not been for my career in education, I would not have experienced being MENTORED as I continued my education while LEADING others. I've spent 31 years in education working to encourage, inspire, became a teacher and after many promotions eventually becoming an area superintendent. In my growth and aspirations, I'm working on LIVING THE LEGACY I want to leave and providing a blueprint of what a successful career can look like. Intentional Mentoring is the LIVING LEGACY I choose to leave you, my community, and the world as I strive to make life better for all mankind one mentor-mentee relationship at a time. It is the path I was created to take, and one I take pleasure in sharing with you.

Sincerely,

Dr. Kenneth D. Davis

The Pillars...

LIVING...
LOVING...
LEARNING...
LAUGHING...
LEADING...
LEGACY...

INTRODUCTION

Throughout the history of humanity, it has become apparent that humans learn better when they participate in peer-to-peer learning opportunities. Mentoring is another aspect of peer-to-peer learning that presents the mentee with the modeling of behavior that leads to successful outcomes and firsthand experiences by identifying the skills and tools exemplified in leaders. Mentoring has become a universal opportunity to build a sense of self, improve personal and/or professional development, create a supportive learning environment, open avenues for exposure to opportunities and possibilities previously unknown, and an emotional support system for both the mentor and the mentee. This is why schools, corporations and organizations have created mentoring programs where leadership mentor's frontline and subordinate employees and/or youth. In schools, it has become even more effective when mentees are paired with educators who share their same ethnic and cultural beliefs.

In every instance, a mentee – whether students in an educational setting or adults in the workplace – benefits from the guidance mentors offer to better understand their pathway when navigating life and gaining knowledge. This is an essential ingredient in their development of their sense of self and when moving towards their purpose as they prepare to make decisions regarding their long-term personal and professional goals. The trust relationship that is built between the mentor and mentee empowers mentees to create a ripple effect, where they become a mentor to a new class of mentees. They take what they learned and experienced as a mentee and create a relationship with their mentee that introduces the mentee to a whole new world of opportunities and possibilities. The effectiveness of mentoring is why 89% of those who were mentored give back and become mentors. (10 Compelling Facts About National Mentoring Month, July 7, 2021, https://halo.com/10-compelling-facts-about-national-mentoring-month/)

The need for mentoring programs has not diminished over time, but because of its benefits for both the mentor and mentee, it is in demand even more. Every mentoring relationship should be viewed as mutually beneficial to both the mentor and mentee as they both seek to become a better version of themselves. Their consistent and positive interactions give them the opportunity to view the world and situations through the other person's eyes. As we cover the six pillars, we will share how each can have a positive impact on the lives of the mentor and mentee, if used correctly to create a stable and sound foundation on which the mentoring relationship is built. Just like with everything else in life, a successful mentoring relationship will be designed with both the mentor's and mentee's individual and collective need to set boundaries, clarify expectations and participate in open communication. This opens the door for the mentee and mentor to take part in and benefit from a rewarding and highly effective mentoring experience.

Why does anyone need a mentor? Many have proclaimed it is because they need the guidance to see beyond their limitations to discover the opportunities and/or possibilities available to them that have the potential of changing their future for the better. Others have said it is because it gives mentees insight into a realm of knowledge that was unknown to them (the mentee) that they can now envision themselves doing and/or living. Tomorrow is not promised to anyone and by having a mentor, the mentee is provided with the needed information to develop a roadmap to live a better life than they believed was available to them especially in situations where the circumstances of their birth, and/or the cultural, racial and/or economic disparities dictates as their only options in life.

A mentor/mentee relationship has the potential of expounding the mentee's mindset from one of limitations, to one that is limitless. What was not considered available to him/her becomes a myriad of possibilities that springs from the mentee's belief that nothing is impossible to him/her. For the mentor, they can introduce the unexpected and the previously thought impossible to their mentee and are afforded the unique opportunity to view the world through their mentee's eyes.

To truly see and experience the mentee's life in a way that empowers them to offer hope where only despair and hopelessness existed, is the reality many mentors in youth-based programs experience. By preparing the mentee for what they may encounter and by training the mentor to introduce the human component into the following lessons, each mentor speaks to their mentee in a way that gives the mentee permission to take part in the conversations, learn the lessons, begin applying the lessons learned to their life, situation and/or circumstances and grow into who they now envision themselves as being. In turn, they become successful, contributing members of society who have learned the importance of reaching back into their community, company, or organization and sharing what they learned as a mentee as they begin their new adventure of being a mentor. Building upon what has been given, taught, and shared with them during their mentee experience.

Life is about living, loving, learning, laughing, leading, and leaving your legacy. Each mentor and mentee live a life that represents what is left behind that says I have lived, learned, shared, and touched lives to help them live their best life now, all while envisioning a world that offers opportunities and possibilities. The following lessons are structured to speak into both the heart, mind, and lives of the mentor and mentee to realize their greatest potential as they envision a life founded on hope and hard work. A life that gives them the permission to take the blinders off and release the scales from their eyes to see what's there openly and honestly, while being vulnerable to the experience so they both walk away with a greater understanding of self and the knowledge that nothing is impossible. One that says if I can believe and conceive it (visualize it) and will do the work, it can become my reality.

This mutually beneficial relationship will equip both the mentor and mentee for the next season in their lives which reminds them never to forget who they once were. To forget is to return to what was and to experience it again. However, growing and sharing the mentor's story of overcoming with others gives the mentees permission to experience the hope that helps others continue growing, living, learning, loving, leading, and living their legacy as well!

PILLAR:

LIVING

PILLAR: LIVING

I was listening to a daily meditation that said, *"Every problem is a gift! Without problems, we would not grow!"* That immediately made me think about mentoring. Why? Because mentoring is an answer to a societal, community, cultural and/or economic problem. It speaks to the lack that is represented in our world, and by implementing a viable mentoring program, the organizers can offer both hope and an answer to each participant's life's question.

Humanity is designed to be in relationship with and to interact with each other. To interact, live and/or experience life as a community and not alone. In this pillar, both the mentor and mentee will learn the importance of living and not merely existing. While implementing and overseeing the Mentoring Project, I witnessed firsthand how the mentor-mentee relationship gave the mentee permission to live and see life beyond the limitations that initially restricted their belief system, value their view of the world and recognize what was available to them.

The mentee was not only able to visualize a different future for themselves, but to begin speaking out loud the life they desire. Sometimes, they saw themselves as doctors, lawyers and/or educators instead of only athletes who uses sports to save them from a dying community and/or culture. Mentees will learn from their mentor that *"Your life is a physical manifestation of what is going on in your mind's eye"* – Unknown. Instead of dying in the streets of the community they were born or raised in, the mentee now can see the opportunities and possibilities available to them. In corporate America, the low-level employee could go from hating their job and struggling to barely put food on the table and barely pay their bills to preparing a roadmap for their future that equips and prepares them to follow their dreams or do something that makes their job exciting and beneficial. All while affording them the opportunity to make a salary conducive to their skills and abilities.

I know you are saying how can I have that component in my mentoring program. You begin with identifying the various limiting beliefs the mentees you will serve carry in their hearts and minds through group discussions, surveys and/or activities/exercises designed to get them to open up and share. Which showcases the need for the program administrator to train the mentors on how to be culturally sensitive and understand how to recognize their biases to ensure they do not negatively impact the mentor-mentee relationship. Train the mentors on the components of open communication and encourage him/her to have open and informative dialogue with their mentee to derive the information they need while the mentee feels safe sharing with the certainty they will be seen or heard.

In most cases, life looks significantly different in the mentor's life than that of the mentee! The differences may be seen in how they live their lives, culturally, economically, racially, etc. Statistically a Caucasian living in the same house design in a predominantly white/Caucasian community property value is 37% higher than one in a predominantly black or community of color. Which in turn, affects the amount of property taxes collected and money available to fund schools and other social services. Thereby, negatively impacting black communities and those of color ensuring there's a distinct difference in the resources and opportunities available to them.

Although these differences and disparities are a part of life, if both the mentor, and mentee are committed to building a strong and respectful mentoring relationship, together they can work through any biases that may be present in both of their lives and viewpoints on life. In 2020 – 2021, there were protests, rallies, and speeches to bring the necessary people to the table to begin the conversations that can impact the lives and lifestyles of many people culturally, racially, and economically. It is in these settings that plans can be made to make conditions better and that promise to bring some equity to the equation that has been in place and is a part of the fabric of America.

The mindset of each of these individuals must change to ensure the conversations become a plan that is implemented. I share that to say the same thing needs to occur during the development of your mentoring program and in designing the lessons that will be the tool you used to effect change and offer hope to both the mentor and mentee who participates in your program. By having the conversations with a cross section of the community you want to impact, you will have the information necessary to impact their lives.

This pillar on living humanizes and puts a face to all races, their lifestyles, and the conditions in which ALL people live. This lesson should help the participants to become more aware of the racial, economic, and cultural disparities people endure daily and become sensitive to them while determining the best way to offer hope and introduce opportunities and possibilities that may not have been considered because the mentee could not see past their current living conditions and personal limitations.

According to Sunshine Parenting, there are "*5 Ways to Teach Kids to Live Life Well*," (www.Sunshine-Parenting.com):

1. ***Unplug for a while each day***. Whereas the article talked about unplugging from social media. I challenge you to take that a step further. Create activities and/or experiences where the mentee can unplug from their communities, daily limitations, homelife, etc. Provide them with time to

experience something different and debrief. During your debriefing time, ask questions to understand how the experience or activity impacted the mentee. This will help to widen their knowledge base while exposing the mentee to experiences and activities they never saw themselves doing or participating in.

2. **Interact with Others**. This step encourages the mentees to maintain, nurture and build relationships. The mentee is to make it a priority to regularly communicate with friends, family and/or loved ones. As well as participate in activities that will encourage them to build new relationships. According to *"Health Benefits of Social Interactions"* (www.mercycare.org), *"spending quality time with friends, loved ones and/or others can lighten their mood and disposition* (better mental health)*, lower the risk of dementia* (encourage good brain health)*, promote a sense of safety, belonging and security and/or provides you with resources to share confidences."*

    Let's take this a step forward and teach the mentee how to make new connections, how to handle themselves when meeting new people, and/or how to build relationships that will equip them with the tools, connections and/or relationships to rise out of their current situations that are steppingstones that have the potential of becoming lifelong friends.

    Corporate America is moving away from the boardroom to closing business deals during dinner or when out having fun. With that in mind, teaching mentors and mentees how to conduct themselves and the proper dining etiquette during a business dinner may help relieve some of the nervousness and give them more confidence to secure the job or close the deal. By ensuring they have the skills that are needed when going after business ownership or corporate jobs is imperative, especially when those skills aren't used in their daily life and activities in their current community. Mentoring can expose the mentee to what is possible based upon what they aspire to be or do. Then create an opportunity to use what they have learned. The experience can be life changing.

3. **Take Care of You** (your mind, body, and soul). Today, more people are sitting and are isolated from working remotely while completing their daily duties on a computer or for students in the physical or virtual classroom. Your physical health is just as important to maintain as maintaining your mental health. Create an atmosphere where it is safe for the mentee and mentor to move through exercises, dance, etc. Something that will get them up and moving around. Find out what kind of dance your mentees are interested in and have someone to come in and teach them a routine. Then create an opportunity for them to perform it. This builds confidence, self-esteem,

and encourages them to try new things. Even for those who have 2 left feet, help them find their spot in the production and/or planning. Whatever you decide, be sure and have them up and moving together, both the mentee and mentor. This will not only improve their health but release those much-needed endorphins to overcome obstacles they encounter in life.

4. ***Learn to manage your time and priorities.*** As I mentioned previously, time is our most valuable asset, or commodity. Learning how to use it will help with eliminating anxiety and feelings of being overwhelmed. I challenge you to have exercises and/or activities that teach organizational and time management skills. As a part of the exercise or activity, teach the importance of taking breaks while studying and/or working. It gives the brain time to refresh. This is also a time to get up and move around to kick off those endorphins to help you remain focused and on task.

    This may also be a time to introduce meditation and/or visualization. Our thoughts form the life we lead and as such we need to show the mentee, the importance of visualizing themselves living the life they want, doing the job or having the career they want and/or running their business. The mind is the core engine that manifests the story each person tells themself. Through visualization, the person can change the narrative based upon the new information they have and visualize themselves being successful while living their best life. Teach them how to create their individual life and stay on track to manifest what they visualized into their reality.

5. ***Figure out what you like.*** Seldomly do people have time to figure out what they want or like. We can more readily tell what we do not want rather than to state what we want. In school and on the job, we are told what to do and if we want this or that what we need or should be doing. Following this process does not teach anyone how to identify those things they believe will bring them happiness and/or ignite the drive to live their best life now. Look for different scenarios, activities, or experiences to help the mentee discover what he/she is passionate about. Give them an opportunity to experience the various hobbies to determine which one they are good at or interested in. This will help them live "…*thriving, vibrant, happy lives.*" And helps them flourish in the moment, and everyday thereafter.

    Give yourself permission to think outside of societal lines and norms. Introduce mentees to the beauty within their community and outside of their communities. If you find graffiti that inspires and that has brought their community together, even if it was because of tragedy. Take them on a field trip to a small art studio or museum that showcases art from today's up and coming artists.

If possible, have the artist visit your group of mentees to share their story and their art. Give them an opportunity to see that everyone's story matters and how they tell it indicates where their passion lies.

This can spark conversations that divulge the mental and emotional story the mentee tells him/herself to give the mentor further insight into how to reach, communicate, and inspire their mentee. The greatest life lessons are taught and learned outside of the classroom. Once again, give yourself permission to be creative to show both the mentor and mentee the importance of living a life that empowers and enables them to show up in their own life!

Week 1 & 2 Activities

YOUTH ACTIVITIES

Introduction/Living/Getting to Know You

LESSON VOCABULARY WORDS

INSTRUCTIONS: Study the vocabulary words listed below for a good understanding of each one.

MENTORING Creed: 6 MENTORING Pillars:

1. **Live-** *every moment with a purpose*
2. **Love-** *beyond words*
3. **Learn-** *something new every day*
4. **Laugh-** *with no regrets*
5. **Lead-** *to inspire others*
6. **Legacy-** *live your legacy*

Discussion Topic: Quote from Dr. Seuss: *"Today you are you! That is truer than true! There is no one alive who is you-er than you!"*

Question: What does this quote mean to you?

_____
_____
_____
_____
_____
_____
_____
_____
_____
_____
_____
_____

Pillar: Living

ACTIVITY: TWO TRUTHS AND A LIE

Share three things about yourself, but two of the statements must be true and one must be a lie. The goal of the game is for the rest of the group to guess which statement is false. For example, you might say, "I play the guitar, I've never been on a plane, and I can't swim." The group will try to guess which of the statements you shared is a lie.

Intentional Mentoring Mentee's Workbook

Let me introduce myself...

Graphic Organizer Activity

SELF PORTRAIT

Favorites
- COLOR: ....
- MOVIE: ....
- FOOD: ....
- CELEBRITY: ....
- SUBJECT: ....
- HOBBY: ....
- SPORT: ....
- MUSIC: ....

Favorite Summer Memory
....
....
....
....

Birthday
_____

Grade
_____

Siblings
_____
_____
_____
_____

The best book I read:
_____
_____
_____

Pets

Biggest Accomplishment
_____
_____
_____
_____
_____

What makes me unique?
_____
_____

What makes a good teacher?

My future plans are...
_____
_____
_____
_____

3 Words that describe me...
1. _____
2. _____
3. _____

Creative Social Skills Activities for Youth

(https://teens.lovetoknow.com/creative-social-skills-activities-teens-tweens)

The following are real life social skills activities:

Stress Reduction Circuit

This activity teaches how to calm yourself down in stressful situations or conversations is a vital social skill. Use the happiness pyramid to measure your results.

1. Find five images of various stages of happiness or write those stages on a piece of paper.
2. Choose 3 to 5 calming techniques like drawing, listening to music, yoga, counting backward from 10, deep breathing exercises, running, or playing basketball.
3. Set up a "station" for each of your chosen calming techniques.
4. Write down something that stresses you out or makes you frustrated. Write down which stage of happiness from the pyramid this action makes you feel.
5. Spend about five minutes doing one of the chosen calming techniques. When time is up, use the happiness pyramid to write down what stage the youth is at.
6. Repeat Step 5 with each calming technique.
7. Identify which of the calming techniques made you feel the happiest? How could you use this knowledge to help you deal with stressful interactions?

Tell which one made you feel the happiest, and how you could use this knowledge to help you deal with stressful interactions you face daily?

Nonverbal Telephone

Practice using and understanding nonverbal communication with this twist on the classic talking game, Telephone.

1. Write a bunch of emotions on slips of paper and put them in a bowl. Emotions include angry, excited, tired, and grumpy.
2. Stand in a line with the other participants facing the back of the person in front of you.
3. The person at the back of the line will secretly draw one emotion.
4. The person at the back of the line will tap the person in front of them. This person should turn around to face whoever tapped them.
5. The person who tapped you will use 3 nonverbal clues to show the emotion, then the person they tapped will turn back around.
6. Each successive player will repeat Steps 4 and 5 using the same or similar nonverbal cues as before.
7. The last person will try to guess the emotion after they see the clues.

EMAIL MADNESS

Make quick decisions about personal versus professional communication.

1. Have an electronic device capable of sending email in real time.
2. Have your email account open on a separate device.
3. The facilitator or mentor will call out a recipient and subject such as "*Dr. Brown, homeopathic suggestions for a headache,*" or "*Grandma, planning Easter.*"
4. You will have five minutes to craft and send your email that fits the scenario provided.
5. After five minutes another scenario will be provided. R*eply* to the previous email you sent so all your answers are in one email thread.

TAKE A VIRTUAL ART TOUR

Critique and discuss the works of art presented and share your opinion and feelings with the group:

1. View each piece of art and share your opinion and feelings with the group. Answer the following when sharing: How does it make you feel? Do you like it? What does it look like to you?

QUESTIONS MENTEES CAN ASK THEIR MENTORS

1. Why did you decide to be a mentor?
2. What are your goals for the relationship?
3. I'm keen to get your input on my goals for this mentorship. Can we review them together?
4. How often do you want to meet?
5. What's your preferred method of communication?
6. How can I better prepare for our meetings?
7. What are your goals for this relationship?
8. Where do you see yourself in 3-5 years?
9. What are your greatest challenges right now?
10. What part of your job most excites you?
11. What motivates you?
12. How are you feeling?
13. What are you excited about right now?
14. What's new since we last spoke?
15. How are you staying motivated?
16. What's a goal you're currently working towards?
17. What's going on outside of work in your life?
18. If someone was writing the story of your career, what would you want it to be?
19. Do you have any advice on how I can approach discussions about a promotion?
20. I feel like I'm being pigeonholed at work right now and would like to try some new things. In your experience, what's the best way to approach this?
21. If you were me, how would you have approached X situation?
22. Do you think I should accept this new job offer?
23. My salary isn't in line with what my peers are making. How do I ask for more?
24. What skills would be beneficial for me to work on?
25. Where do you think I can improve?
26. What could I have done differently in this specific situation that may have improved the outcome?
27. Do you have any recommendations for professional development courses?
28. Are there any good books you can suggest that would help me improve X skill?

https://www.togetherplatform.com/blog/29-questions-to-ask-your-mentor-in-your-next-meeting

JOURNAL PAGES

*A mentor is not someone who walks ahead of you to show you how they did it.
A mentor walks alongside you to show you want you can do.* –Unknown

Pillar: Living

EMPLOYEE/COMMUNITY CITIZEN ACTIVITIES

Pillar: Living

Introduction/Living/Getting to Know You

LESSON VOCABULARY WORDS

INSTRUCTIONS: Study the vocabulary words listed below for a good understanding of each one.

MENTORING Creed: 6 MENTORING Pillars:

1. *Live-* every moment with a purpose
2. *Love-* beyond words
3. *Learn-* something new every day
4. *Laugh-* with no regrets
5. *Lead-* to inspire others
6. *Legacy-* live your legacy

Discussion Topic: Quote from Dr. Seuss: *"Today you are you! That is truer than true! There is no one alive who is you-er than you!"*

Question: What does this quote mean to you?

_____
_____
_____
_____
_____
_____
_____
_____
_____
_____
_____

QUESTIONS MENTEES CAN ASK THEIR MENTORS

1. Why did you decide to be a mentor?
2. What are your goals for the relationship?
3. I'm keen to get your input on my goals for this mentorship. Can we review them together?
4. How often do you want to meet?
5. What's your preferred method of communication?
6. How can I better prepare for our meetings?
7. What are your goals for this relationship?
8. Where do you see yourself in 3-5 years?
9. What are your greatest challenges right now?
10. What part of your job most excites you?
11. What motivates you?
12. How are you feeling?
13. What are you excited about right now?
14. What's new since we last spoke?
15. How are you staying motivated?
16. What's a goal you're currently working towards?
17. What's going on outside of work in your life?
18. If someone was writing the story of your career, what would you want it to be?
19. Do you have any advice on how I can approach discussions about a promotion?
20. I feel like I'm being pigeonholed at work right now and would like to try some new things. In your experience, what's the best way to approach this?
21. If you were me, how would you have approached X situation?
22. Do you think I should accept this new job offer?
23. My salary isn't in line with what my peers are making. How do I ask for more?
24. What skills would be beneficial for me to work on?
25. Where do you think I can improve?
26. What could I have done differently in this specific situation that may have improved the outcome?
27. Do you have any recommendations for professional development courses?
28. Are there any good books you can suggest that would help me improve X skill?

https://www.togetherplatform.com/blog/29-questions-to-ask-your-mentor-in-your-next-meeting

Pillar: Living

Let me introduce myself...

Graphic Organizer Activity

JOURNAL PAGES

Pillar: Living

Week 3 & 4 Activities

YOUTH ACTIVITIES

Pillar: Living

Reaching My Goals

LESSON VOCABULARY WORDS

INSTRUCTIONS: Review vocabulary and ensure you have a good understanding of each one.

1. **Goal:** An aim or desired result.
2. **Short-term:** Relating to or extending over a limited period.
3. **Long-term:** Things that are so enduring that they're nearly permanent.

Discussion Question: What are you going to do today, tomorrow, and next week to get closer to your goal?"

PARTICIPANT INFORMATION WORKSHEET

Name: _____

Organization: _____ Date: _____

What name do you prefer to be called? _____

Do you have a nickname? _____

What are your three favorite subjects... why?
1. _____ because _____
2. _____ because _____
3. _____ because _____

What do you like to do in your spare time (LIST 3 THINGS)
Besides EAT and SLEEP
_____
_____
_____

> Favorite kind of music? _____
> 2 of your favorite songs right now? _____
> _____

Do you or anyone in your family speak any languages besides English?
Yes (who) _____ No _____
If so, what languages? _____

Where is the farthest away from home you have ever been? _____

What activities are you involved in at the school? (Sports, music, clubs, etc.) _____
_____

Tell me something interesting about you.... _____
_____

Is there anything else I should know about you? (Medical issues? Left-handed? Very shy? Good with computers?) _____
_____

Have you been a part of a mentoring program before? Yes ____ No ____
If yes, which program and for how long? _____

What OBSTACLES do you see in your present life that might make it more difficult to REACH your goals? _____
_____

If you had the opportunity to work with a mentor, what would be your objectives for that relationship? Circle all that apply.

☐ Career advice & development   ☐ Work on Math Skills
☐ Improve Reading   ☐ Help with Science
☐ Improve Writing   ☐ Help with Social Studies
☐ Learn Leadership Skills   ☐ Help with Health
☐ Learn About College   ☐ Have someone to talk to
☐ Learn/Practice Another
   Language

Please circle all applicable options that describe you.

Considerate   Outgoing   Serious   Efficient   Friendly

Convincing   Organized   Independent   Agreeable

Responsible   Authoritative   Helpful   Enthusiastic   Precise

Pillar: Living

MENTEE AGREEMENT

As a mentee with the _____ Mentoring Program, I agree to the following:

1. To meet regularly with my mentor
2. To be on time for scheduled meetings
3. To notify the mentor if I cannot keep my weekly meeting
4. To engage in the relationship with an open mind
5. To accept assistance from my mentor
6. To keep discussions with my mentor confidential
7. To practice skills and behaviors taught to me by my mentor

Acknowledgement of Program Expectations (Please initial by each line)

_____ I have read and understand the overall mission/vision of the _____ Mentoring Program Objectives.

_____ I understand what is expected of me as a mentee

_____ I understand I should put forth an effort to practice new skills and behaviors

_____ I am willing to continue working with my mentee after the scheduled program timeline

Mentee (Print Name) _____

Signature: _____ Date: _____

UNDERSTANDING GOALS

The main thing to remember is that today's youth's goals must be their own, not goals anyone else has set for them. Even extremely lofty goals should be respected, and you can show your mentee how to break down that goal into smaller steps on the way to reaching the goal. For example, a good education is an important first step in becoming president of a corporation. Perhaps more to the point, doing tonight's homework is the first step toward getting a good education.

CHARACTERISTICS GOALS SHOULD HAVE

- *Conceivable*: The mentee should be able to define his/her goal and see it clearly, so he/she can understand what the steps are to achieve it.

- *Believable*: The mentee must believe he/she can reach their goal.

- *Achievable*: The goals the mentee sets must be within his/her strengths and abilities. For example, someone who has never lifted weights before probably should not set a goal of a 300 lb. bench press by next week. (That could be an achievable long-term goal.)

- *Controllable*: To the extent possible, the mentee's ability to reach their goal should not depend on anyone else. For example, getting a job may depend on the job market and your mentee's parents' approval. However, talking to his/her parents about getting a job or developing a resume are things your mentee can control.

- *Measurable*: The goal should be measurable by a certain time or quantity. If the goal is to get an "A" in algebra, then the mentee should know what grades he/she needs to get on tests and assignments.

- *Desirable*: The goal should be something your mentee really wants to do, not something he/she feels they must do, or should do. For example, earning a living is something that we must do, while learning to play baseball may be something we would like to do.

- *Help you grow*: The goal should never be self-destructive or be destructive towards others, their community and/or society. Help your mentee to distinguish between constructive and destructive goals.

PLANNING FOR ACTION

After you finish identifying your goals, talk about an action plan. It prepares you for the difficulties you might face. Use the following for further discussion:

- ☐ What actions are needed to reach the goal
- ☐ Who will take those actions (if someone besides the youth is involved)
- ☐ When will the actions be taken
- ☐ What resources are needed in support of the action
- ☐ What difficulties will your mentee face, and their possible solutions
- ☐ Encourage your mentee to talk to about his/her plans

https://ctb.ku.edu/en/table-of-contents/implement/youth-mentoring/youth-goal-setting/main

POPULAR GOALS YOUTH HAVE

- Lose Weight
- Set up a budget
- Start journaling
- Drink More Water
- Graduate High School
- Build good study habits
- Learn a new language
- Apply to college
- Save money
- Learn to play an instrument
- Get more sleep
- Do something I have never done
- Complete a driver's ed course
- Read more
- Join a school club organization
- Make 3 new friends
- Exercise more
- Practice gratitude

GOAL

Education

Career

Health

Financial

Family

Personal Pleasure

REACHING MY GOALS

What to do: Think of some of your personal goals. Try to think of 5. Write the goal. Beside the goal write what type of goal it is. Be prepared to discuss your goals with your mentor.

Goal #1: _____

                                                          Type of goal: _____

Goal #2: _____

                                                          Type of goal: _____

Goal #3: _____

                                                          Type of goal: _____

Goal #4: _____

                                                          Type of goal: _____

Goal #5: _____

                                                          Type of goal: _____

EMPLOYEE/COMMUNITY CITIZEN ACTIVITIES

Reaching My Goals

LESSON VOCABULARY WORDS

INSTRUCTIONS: Study the vocabulary words listed below for a good understanding of each one.

1. **Goal:** An aim or desired result.
2. **Short-term:** Relating to or extending over a limited period.
3. **Long-term:** Things that are so enduring that they're nearly permanent.

Discussion Question: What are you going to do today, tomorrow, and next week to get closer to your goal?"

_____
_____
_____
_____
_____
_____
_____
_____
_____
_____
_____
_____
_____
_____
_____
_____
_____

PARTICIPANT INFORMATION WORKSHEET

Name: _____

Organization: _____ Date: _____

What name do you prefer to be called? _____

Do you have a nickname? _____

What are your three favorite subjects... why?

1. _____ because _____
2. _____ because _____
3. _____ because _____

What do you like to do in your spare time (LIST 3 THINGS) Besides EAT and SLEEP

| Favorite kind of music? _____ |
| 2 of your favorite songs right now? _____ |

Do you or anyone in your family speak any languages besides English?
Yes (who) _____ No _____
If so, what languages? _____

Where is the farthest away from home you have ever been? _____

What activities are you involved in at the school? (Sports, music, clubs, etc.) _____

Tell me something interesting about you... _____

Is there anything else I should know about you? (Medical issues? Left-handed? Very shy? Good with computers?) _____

Have you been a part of a mentoring program before? Yes ___ No ___
If yes, which program and for how long? _____

What OBSTACLES do you see in your present life that might make it more difficult to REACH your goals? _____

If you had the opportunity to work with a mentor, what would be your objectives for that relationship? Circle all that apply.

- ☐ Career advice & development
- ☐ Improve Reading
- ☐ Improve Writing
- ☐ Learn Leadership Skills
- ☐ Learn About College
- ☐ Learn/Practice Another Language
- ☐ Work on Math Skills
- ☐ Help with Science
- ☐ Help with Social Studies
- ☐ Help with Health
- ☐ Have someone to talk to

Please circle all applicable options that describe you.

Considerate   Outgoing   Serious   Efficient   Friendly

Convincing   Organized   Independent   Agreeable

Responsible   Authoritative   Helpful   Enthusiastic   Precise

MENTEE AGREEMENT

As a mentee with the _____ Mentoring Program, I agree to the following:

1. To meet regularly with my mentor
2. To be on time for scheduled meetings
3. To notify the mentor if I cannot keep my weekly meeting
4. To engage in the relationship with an open mind
5. To accept assistance from my mentor
6. To keep discussions with my mentor confidential
7. To practice skills and behaviors taught to me by my mentor

Acknowledgement of Program Expectations (Please initial by each line)

_____   I have read and understand the overall mission/vision of the _____ Mentoring Program Objectives.

_____   I understand what is expected of me as a mentee

_____   I understand I should put forth an effort to practice new skills and behaviors

_____   I am willing to continue working with my mentee after the scheduled program timeline

Mentee (Print Name) _____

Signature: _____   Date: _____

Pillar: Living

SMART GOALS

Make it specific

In order for a goal to be effective, it needs to be specific. A specific goal answers questions like: What needs to be accomplished? Who's responsible for it? What steps need to be taken to achieve it? Thinking through these questions helps get to the heart of what you're aiming for.

Make it measurable

Specificity is a solid start, but quantifying your goals (that is, making sure they're measurable) makes it easier to track progress and know when you've reached the finish line. To make this SMART objective more impactful, Jane should incorporate measurable and trackable benchmarks.

Make it attainable

This is the point in the process when you give yourself a serious reality check. Goals should be realistic — not pedestals from which you inevitably tumble. Ask yourself: is your objective something you can reasonably accomplish?

Make it relatable

Here's where you need to think about the big picture. Why are you setting the goal that you're setting? Consider your objective.

Make it timely

To properly measure success, you need to on the goal and determine when it can be reached. What's your time horizon? When will you start creating and implementing the tasks you've identified? When will you finish? SMART goals should have time-related parameters built in, so you know how to stay on track within a designated time frame.

https://www.atlassian.com/blog/productivity/how-to-write-smart-goals

Intentional Mentoring Mentee's Workbook

GOAL SETTING

WHAT IS YOUR GOAL?

_____

_____

_____

_____

ACTION STEPS

01 _____

02 _____

03 _____

04 _____

START DATE: DEADLINE: MARK COMPLETE:

Pillar: Living

MONTHLY GOALS

MONTH :

FOCUS

GOAL

ACTIONS STEPS

GOAL

ACTIONS STEPS

GOAL

ACTIONS STEPS

TASK LIST

NOTES

Goal Setting

Goals	Action Steps

Problems	

Progress Tracker

Date	Progress

Pillar: Living

setting goals

MY PRIORITIES
1.
2.
3.
4.
5.

When I feel like giving up, I will tell myself…

GOAL: _____
Action Steps-
1.
2.
3.
DEADLINE: _____

GOAL: _____
Action Steps-
1.
2.
3.
DEADLINE: _____

GOAL: _____
Action Steps-
1.
2.
3.
DEADLINE: _____

GOAL: _____
Action Steps-
1.
2.
3.
DEADLINE: _____

GOAL: _____
Action Steps-
1.
2.
3.
DEADLINE: _____

Week at a Glance   PLAN DO REVIEW

TOP 3 GOALS OF THE _____
1.
2.
3.

APPOINTMENTS & EVENTS

TO DO
- [ ]
- [ ]
- [ ]
- [ ]
- [ ]
- [ ]
- [ ]

BOOK I'M READING

SKILL I'M PRACTICING

HABITS
	S	M	T	W	T	F	S

INCOME GOAL // SAVINGS GOAL

END OF WEEK REVIEW

WHAT WORKED?	WHAT DIDN'T WORK?
DO MORE:	DO LESS:
GRATITUDE:	EPIPHANY:

get the whole kit at: www.bit.ly/lifebinder

Week 5 & 6 Activities

YOUTH ACTIVITIES

Pillar: Living

Developing Meaningful Relationships

LESSON VOCABULARY WORDS

INSTRUCTIONS: Study the vocabulary words listed below for a good understanding of each one.

1. **Relationships:** The way in which two or more concepts, objects, or people are connected, or the state of being connected.
2. **Development:** Process of improvement and changes required for better living and existence.
3. **Self-Awareness:** become mindful; acknowledge what you need rather than what you want; set boundaries
4. **Relationship Skills:** forgive; guiding love
5. **Purpose:** the reason for which something is done, created, or exists

List some of the benefits of having/developing relationships (examples: Someone is there for you, love and companionship, safety, sharing culture, religion, challenges, and/or someone to just have fun with.)

Healthy Relationships	Unhealthy Relationships

Discussion Questions: Be prepared to answer these questions during the open discussion time with the group.

1. What does a healthy relationship look like?

_____
_____
_____

2. What does an unhealthy relationship look like?

   _____
   _____
   _____

3. How do you know the difference?

   _____
   _____
   _____

4. Why do some people stay in unhealthy relationships?

   _____
   _____
   _____

ATTITUDE OF GRATITUDE: The positive relationships you currently have in your life impact how you see life and interact with the world around you. Tell the people you are in a healthy relationship with how grateful you are for the relationship. Take the opportunity to share your gratitude towards someone, in a written message, and/or by using technology.

EMPLOYEE/COMMUNITY CITIZEN ACTIVITIES

Developing Meaningful Relationships

LESSON VOCABULARY WORDS

INSTRUCTIONS: Study the vocabulary words listed below for a good understanding of each one.

1. **Relationships:** The way in which two or more concepts, objects, or people are connected, or the state of being connected.
2. **Development:** Process of improvement and changes required for better living and existence.
3. **Self-Awareness:** become mindful; acknowledge what you need rather than what you want; set boundaries
4. **Relationship Skills:** forgive; guiding love
5. **Purpose:** the reason for which something is done, created, or exists

List some of the benefits of having/developing relationships (examples: Someone is there for you, love and companionship, safety, sharing culture, religion, challenges, and/or someone to just have fun with.)

Healthy Relationships	Unhealthy Relationships

Discussion Questions: Be prepared to answer these questions during the open discussion time with the group.

1. What does a healthy relationship look like?

_____
_____
_____

Pillar: Living

2. What does an unhealthy relationship look like?

   _____
   _____
   _____

3. How do you know the difference?

   _____
   _____
   _____

4. Why do some people stay in unhealthy relationships?

   _____
   _____
   _____

ATTITUDE OF GRATITUDE: The positive relationships you currently have in your life impact how you see life and interact with the world around you. Tell the people you are in a healthy relationship with how grateful you are for the relationship. Take the opportunity to share your gratitude for a person, in a written message, and/or by using technology.

Week 7 & 8 Activities

YOUTH ACTIVITIES

Legacy/Cultural EYE

LESSON VOCABULARY WORDS

INSTRUCTIONS: Study the vocabulary words listed below for a good understanding of each one.

1. **Culture:** The customary beliefs, social forms, and material traits of a racial, religious, or social group.
2. **Ethnicity:** The fact or state of belonging to a social group that has a common national or cultural tradition.
3. **Race:** Each of the major groupings into which humankind is considered (in various theories or contexts) to be divided on the basis of physical characteristics or shared ancestry.
4. **Stereotype:** A widely held but fixed and oversimplified image or idea of a particular type of person or thing.
5. **Discrimination:** The unjust or prejudicial treatment of different categories of people or things, especially on the grounds of race, age, or sex
6. **Bias**: a disproportionate weight in favor of or against an idea or thing, usually in a way that is closed-minded, prejudicial, or unfair.

Discussion Questions: Be prepared to answer these questions during the group's discussion period.

1. What is culture?
   _____
   _____
   _____

2. What is bias?
   _____
   _____
   _____

3. How does culture and bias play out in the workplace or in the community?
   _____
   _____
   _____

4. What does acceptance and inclusion mean?
   _____
   _____
   _____

Pillar: Living

5. What is bias?
   _____
   _____
   _____

During the Cultural Representations Presentation answer the following questions:

a. What is being shared? _____
   _____
   _____

b. What culture is being representing? _____
   _____
   _____

c. What did you take away from this cultural tradition? _____
   _____
   _____

d. Where did the cultural tradition originate? Place a marker on the map for each region or area represented. _____
   _____
   _____

e. Write down two examples of diverse cultural traditions in your community, or within your family.
   _____
   _____
   _____

"Culture is a shared set of practices and traditions that characterize a society or group of people. Culture can include clothing, food, traditions, rituals, ceremonies, spiritual practices, and beliefs, language, family structure, and communication styles. Celebrating a diversity of cultural traditions promotes tolerance and understanding. Cultural beliefs/values impact the legacy you desire to leave the world because they are infused in your core values and beliefs."

EMPLOYEE/COMMUNITY CITIZEN ACTIVITIES

Pillar: Living

Legacy/Cultural EYE

LESSON VOCABULARY WORDS

INSTRUCTIONS: Study the vocabulary words listed below for a good understanding of each one.

1. **Culture:** The customary beliefs, social forms, and material traits of a racial, religious, or social group.
2. **Ethnicity:** The fact or state of belonging to a social group that has a common national or cultural tradition.
3. **Race:** Each of the major groupings into which humankind is considered (in various theories or contexts) to be divided on the basis of physical characteristics or shared ancestry.
4. **Stereotype:** A widely held but fixed and oversimplified image or idea of a particular type of person or thing.
5. **Discrimination:** The unjust or prejudicial treatment of different categories of people or things, especially on the grounds of race, age, or sex.
6. **Bias:** a disproportionate weight in favor of or against an idea or thing, usually in a way that is closed-minded, prejudicial, or unfair.

Discussion Questions: Be prepared to answer these questions during the group's discussion period.

1. What is culture?

   _____
   _____
   _____

2. What is bias?

   _____
   _____
   _____

3. How does culture and bias play out in the workplace or in the community?

   _____
   _____
   _____

4. What does acceptance and inclusion mean?

   _____
   _____
   _____

5. What is legacy?
   _____
   _____
   _____

6. What part does culture play in legacy?
   _____
   _____
   _____

Reflection: Culture is a shared set of practices and traditions that characterize a society or group of people. Culture can include clothing, food, traditions, rituals, ceremonies, spiritual practices, and beliefs, language, family structure, and communication styles. Celebrating a diversity of cultural traditions promotes tolerance and understanding. Cultural beliefs/values impact the legacy you desire to leave the world because they are infused in your core values and beliefs.

PILLAR:

LOVING

PILLAR: LOVING

Merriam's Dictionary defines love as a strong affection for another arising out of kinship or personal ties; attention based on affection and tenderness; affection based on admiration, benevolence, or common interest. As we understand love, we must first begin with the most important aspect of love: self-love, before moving to loving entities outside of ourselves. According to "*Self-Love and What it Means,*" (www.bbrfoundation.org, February 12, 2020), self-love is a state of appreciation for oneself that grows from actions that support our physical, psychological, and spiritual growth. Self-love means having a high regard for your own well-being and happiness (above that of others). Self-love means taking care of your own needs and not sacrificing your happiness and/or wellbeing to please others. Knowing your value and worth is what self-love is all about. Self-love means not settling for less than you deserve.

In the "*A Seven Step Prescription for Self-love*" article (www.psychologytoday.com, by Deborah Khoshaba, PsyD., 3/27/2012), there are seven steps to cultivate self-love:

1. ***Become Mindful***. Take a minute and take the pulse of your self-love. Be mindful of who you believe yourself to be and act on this knowledge rather than focusing more on what others want for you. This connects with the mentee's lesson on living (discovering what he/she is passionate about) while learning how to make themself the most important person in their life. It is easier for him/her to discover their passions when they become mindful of who they are and are respecting and loving of themselves.

2. ***Acknowledge what you need rather than what you want***. When a person learns to practice self-love, they can turn away from things that don't serve them, even if it looks and feel good or are emotionally gratifying. The person can focus on those things that are needed "*...to stay strong, centered, and moving forward in their life...*" By staying focused on what you need,

you turn away from automatic behavior patterns that get you into trouble, stuck in the past, connected to things designed to destroy you and/or encourages self-destructive behaviors/actions.

3. ***Set Boundaries to Protect Yourself***. In the article it states that a person who practices setting personal and professional boundaries will set limits on activities that deplete or harm them physically, emotionally, professionally, and spiritually or that poorly expressed who he/she is publicly and/or privately. It will help them correctly select and bring the right people into their life, especially those who are invited in to be a part of their inner circle. Having and building solid self-love enables and empowers him/her to remove those individuals who find pleasure in his/her pain and loss rather than their success and happiness even if the person is a family member. Learning how to love from a distance will give him/her the space they need to focus on themself and their needs.

4. ***FORGIVE***. It seems like one of the hardest things to do in life is to forgive oneself for those things they have done or taken part in that have not serviced them and/or improved their view of themself. As humans, we seem to punish ourselves instead of accepting responsibility and forgiving ourselves. When practicing self-love, he/she must accept their humanness and their propensity to mess up every now and then. Learning to offer themself some forgiveness for not being perfect but cognizant of who they are. Remember there are no failures if he/she has learned and grown from their mistakes; they are only lessons learned.

5. ***Live Intentionally and Purposefully***. Live your life with purpose, and intentionally. While discovering your purpose, live a meaningful and healthy life. The decisions and choices you make will support this intention and help you see yourself in a positive light. It will help you

learn how to love yourself even more when you see yourself accomplishing your goals and building a better life for yourself.

Helping both the mentor and mentee understand and begin practicing self-love will help them envision the life they want because now they see themselves as being worthy of having it. This is where setting personal goals, mapping them out, and celebrating their attainment is essential to their continued growth and development. Because it speaks to the love, they display or show themselves daily. When they learn the importance of loving themselves, it impacts how they talk to themselves and the mental dialogue they have with themselves. I once heard that "*...when you speak, I AM the unconscious mind says, 'you are so!'*" (*The I Am Principe*, by Charles Ogada, Published 2011) and moves behind the scenes to make what you have spoken to manifest itself in your reality. One important aspect of learning how to love ourselves empowers us to become kinder to ourselves and begin to speak about the future we desire in love and lovingly.

As the person learns how to love themselves, they can love and respect others in a manner that enables them to accept them where they are without it having a negative impact on them. The greatest gift one human can give another is love. As we take a deeper dive into loving as it relates to the relationships we nurture through love and respect, it is important that our personal definition represents the love we experienced early in life. The love that was shown within the family and village/community that helped to raise you or the lack thereof. However, it isn't the same, but it is the foundation on which we build self-love and the guiding love and respect that is developed in the mentor-mentee relationship and is being nurtured. The greatest gift a human can give another is LOVE.

As we take a deeper dive into loving as it relates to relationships, we nurture through love and respect. It is important that our personal definition is impacted by the love we experienced early in life. The love that was shown within the family and village/community that helped raise you or the lack thereof. This lesson rebuilds or renovates the foundation on which self-love, guiding love and respect are built as the mentor/mentee relationship is being nurtured.

GUIDING LOVE

Guiding love offers guidance from a mentor to the mentee and from mentee to mentor in the sharing of different aspects of their life, sharing their likes and dislikes, skills, abilities and/or areas of expertise and/or knowledge that exposes the mentee to opportunities and possibilities they otherwise would not have known is available to him/her. For the mentor, it gives him/her insight into how to best communicate and interact with their mentee. As well as giving the mentor the opportunity to realize the influences, hinderances and/or mindset of their mentee.

This type of love is founded on respect and a genuine desire for both parties to grow and succeed in life. The guiding-love shown from a mentor to a mentee opens them up to recognizes the need in their life to build a structured relationship through which the mentee benefits from receiving advice, wisdom, and instruction from a seasoned, caring, and engaging individual (mentor). All while gaining the awareness, respect and care when building the mentor-mentee relationship and interacting with people.

While researching guiding-love I discovered it is an aspect of agape love, an aspect of the five love languages kept showing up, and integral when building and nurturing any kind of relationship. Yes, even the guiding-love we have been discussing. The following is how it would be conceptualized in the mentor-mentee relationship: words of affirmation, quality time, acts of service, receiving gifts, and physical contact.

Pillar: Loving

Scott Aoki says, *"I believe the love languages have a place in all human relationships and should play an active role in how we communicate as mentors and mentees."* He also states, *"…the connection between a mentor and mentee can be a multifaceted mix of other personal and professional interactions… therefore it follows its own rules regarding personal interactions and open communication."*

1. **WORDS OF AFFIRMATION**

   Words of affirmation include celebratory compliments that are shared after the mentor and/or mentee has accomplished an achievement or goal. It also includes moments when encouragement is needed, and/or when using a salutation and/or sharing one's opinion.

2. **QUALITY TIME**

   One of the most valuable assets a person has is time. Spending quality time when building the mentor/mentee relationship is paramount. What makes it quality time? When both the mentor and mentee attempt to make the time productive. It helps build confidence individually and collectively. Sometimes a kind or encouraging word said during a scheduled or impromptu interaction can be the difference between life and death.

3. **ACTS OF SERVICE**

   Throughout the mentoring relationship, there will be opportunities where the mentor may expose the mentee or vice versa to something that inspire, empower and/or enables them to see life differently. It is found when they take part in community service projects and/or do something unexpected yet encouraging that builds another person's self-esteem. Keep in mind, acts of service within the mentoring relationship builds trust and respect. The act of service can be something small yet impactful or big, and thoughtful. Whichever it is, it speaks of the reverence and respect being developed between the mentor and mentee, and others.

4. **PHYSICAL TOUCH**

   This type of love language can be seen as too much for some, however, it is necessary even when building a supportive and respectful mentoring relationship. I am talking about something kind and innocent: a part on the back, high-five, a handshake, an encouraging smile and/or eye contact during a conversation. These all can offer a level of communication between two people that encourages them to be and do better.

5. **RECEIVING GIFTS**

   At first glance, most people would say this love language is inappropriate in a mentoring program. I challenge that thought! Merriam-Webster's dictionary defines a gift or present as an item given to someone without the expectation of payment or anything in return. Giving the gift of knowledge, understanding, acceptance, skills, tools, examples to right living, and/or being seen are invaluable to the person receiving it. It isn't about the gift itself or the person receiving it, as much as it is about the recipient (mentee) receiving it, opening it, and using it. Under this guise, giving gifts from mentor to mentee is not only necessary but required to ensure the mentee receives the pertinent information that fosters their mentor-mentee relationship, and equips the mentee with the information, tools, and/or skills to make wise choices and/or decisions in their life during the various stages of their growth and/or development personally and professionally.

The interpretation and use of these five love languages ensures both the mentor and mentee are benefiting from the mentoring relationship. It helps to shape their lives by going forward while encouraging them to show the best version of themselves each day. Love is an essential ingredient in human development and is essential when developing/building a mentoring relationship.

Week 9 & 10 Activities

YOUTH ACTIVITIES

Self-Love/Critical Thinking/Boundaries

LESSON VOCABULARY WORDS

INSTRUCTIONS: Study the vocabulary words listed below for a good understanding of each one.

1. **Love:** a strong affection for another arising out of kinship or personal ties; attention based on affection and tenderness; affection based on admiration, benevolence, or common interests.

2. **Personal Boundaries:** are the limits and rules we set for ourselves within relationships.

3. **Forgiveness:** a conscious, deliberate decision to release feelings of resentment or vengeance toward a person or group who has harmed you, regardless of whether they actually deserve your forgiveness.

Discussion Questions: Be prepared to answer the following questions during the group's discussion time.

1. What is Critical Thinking?
   _____
   _____

2. What are the components of critical thinking?
   _____
   _____

3. Who will you go to for help if your boundaries are not being respected at home, school, church, etc.?
   _____
   _____

4. What will you say to an adult/friend who does not respect your boundaries?
   _____
   _____

5. How can you tell what someone's personal boundaries are regarding personal space and/or touch?
   _____
   _____

6. How will you respect another person's boundaries?
   _____
   _____

Pillar: Loving

Activity: *"How Many Can You Think Of?"* Facilitator/Mentor will think of 1-2 words that fits into a theme or category during the group's discussion period to write down as many words that are related to the theme or category the word belongs to.

BOUNDARIES WORKSHEET – EMOTIONAL BOUNDARIES

INSTRUCTIONS: Emotional boundaries of an individual are his thoughts, feelings, and cognitions that separate him from the thoughts, feelings, and cognitions of others. In the table given below, state some of your emotional boundaries and how they differ from those of others. Brainstorm and write down the healthy ways in which you would react if somebody tried to cross your emotional boundaries.

Emotional Boundaries	Difference from Other's Emotional Boundaries	My Reaction if Someone Violates my Emotional Boundaries

https://optimistminds.com/boundaries-worksheets/

Pillar: Loving

BOUNDARIES WORKSHEET – PERSONAL BOUNDARIES

INSTRUCTIONS: In the table given below, write down some of the healthy boundaries in your relationship and think of ways in which you can improve them further. In the next table, recall and write down the unhealthy boundaries to your relationship. Mention the ways in which you can replace them with healthy boundaries.

Healthy Boundaries in My Relationships	Ways to Improve Them

Unhealthy Boundaries in My Relationships	Ways to Replace Them with Healthy Ones

https://optimistminds.com/boundaries-worksheets/

BOUNDARIES WORKSHEET – PERSONAL BOUNDARIES

INSTRUCTIONS: Personal boundaries of an individual define his/her likes and dislikes, personal beliefs, emotions, etc. in the table given below write down your personal boundaries and the way, you would tell others about these. Also, mention the ways your boundaries can be violated and your reaction in that case.

Personal Boundaries	How do I communicate these Others	How Someone Can Violate my Personal Boundaries	My Reaction When Someone Violates my Boundaries

https://optimistminds.com/boundaries-worksheets/

EMPLOYEE OR COMMUNITY CITIZEN ACTIVITIES

Self-Love/Critical Thinking/Boundaries

LESSON VOCABULARY WORDS

INSTRUCTIONS: Study the vocabulary words listed below for a good understanding of each one.

1. **Critical Thinking:** helps people make good decisions, understand the consequences of their actions, and solve problems.
2. **Facts:** statements that can be verified.
3. **Opinions:** statements that express a person's feelings, attitudes, or beliefs.
4. **Boundaries:** limits people set to protect themselves from being hurt, manipulated, or taken advantage of; personal limits.
5. **Love:** an intense feeling of deep affection.

Discussion Question:

1. What is Critical Thinking?

    _____
    _____

2. What are the components of critical thinking?

    _____
    _____

3. What is the difference between facts and opinions?

    _____
    _____
    _____
    _____

4. What are boundaries?

    _____
    _____

5. What are core values?

    _____
    _____

Pillar: Loving

6. In what way can facts and opinions impact your core values?

7. How will you maintain your boundaries when they are not being respected at home, work/school, church, etc.?

8. What will you say to an adult/friend/family-member who does not respect your boundaries?

9. How can you tell when you have unintentionally crossed someone's personal boundaries?

Fact vs. Opinion

1. *Locating Judgment Words.* (*Underline or circle the bias or qualifying words.*):
    1. Purchasing a brand-new car is a terrible waste of money.
    2. I hate or love my job and the company I work for.
    3. Marvel Comics are better than DC Comics, especially Luke Cage and the Black Panther.
    4. The new iPhone I purchased came with a set of ear-buds.
    5. Volunteers for Habitat for Humanity are engaged in a worthwhile activity.

2. *Distinguishing Between Fact and Opinion in a Paragraph.*
   [1] Flowering plants that are native to the South include purple coneflower and rose verbena. [2] In the view of many longtime gardeners, these two plants are an essential part of the Southern landscape. [3] Trees that are native to the South include a variety of oaks, as well as flowering dogwoods and redbuds. [4] Dogwoods are especially lovely, with their white, pink, or coral blossoms announcing the arrival of spring. [5] For fall color, the deep red of the Virginia willow makes a spectacular show in the native Southern Garden.

   1. _____   2. _____   3. _____

   4. _____   5. _____

Activity: Write down your ten most important values and answer the questions for each value.

1. _____

    a. What will I allow given this value: _____

    b. What will I tolerate given this value: _____

    c. What will I NOT allow given this value: _____

2. _____

    a. What will I allow given this value: _____

    b. What will I tolerate given this value: _____

    c. What will I NOT allow given this value: _____

3. _____

    a. What will I allow given this value: _____

    b. What will I tolerate given this value: _____

    c. What will I NOT allow given this value: _____

4. _____

    a. What will I allow given this value: _____

    b. What will I tolerate given this value: _____

Pillar: Loving

  c. What will I NOT allow given this value: _____
_____

5. _____
  a. What will I allow given this value: _____
_____

  b. What will I tolerate given this value: _____
_____

  c. What will I NOT allow given this value: _____
_____

6. _____
  a. What will I allow given this value: _____
_____

  b. What will I tolerate given this value: _____
_____

  c. What will I NOT allow given this value: _____
_____

7. _____
  a. What will I allow given this value: _____
_____

  b. What will I tolerate given this value: _____
_____

  c. What will I NOT allow given this value: _____
_____

8. _____
  a. What will I allow given this value: _____
_____

  b. What will I tolerate given this value: _____

c. What will I NOT allow given this value: _____

_____

9. _____

   a. What will I allow given this value: _____

   _____

   b. What will I tolerate given this value: _____

   _____

   c. What will I NOT allow given this value: _____

   _____

9. _____

   a. What will I allow given this value: _____

   _____

   b. What will I tolerate given this value: _____

   _____

   c. What will I NOT allow given this value: _____

   _____

FIND YOUR CORE VALUES

Activity: In your relationship, your values may include having shared interests or working towards common goals. At work, your values may include having a healthy work-life balance or a strong company culture. Your family values may include spending quality time together or even limiting the amount of time spent together.

1. Write down your ten most important values, then narrow them down to 3 or 4 core values. These will help you determine what you can accept or tolerate and what you will not accept in any given situation.

2. For each core value, ask yourself the following 3 questions and write down your answers:

   a. What will I allow given this value?
   b. What will I tolerate given this value?
   c. What will I not allow given this value?

3. Learn how to clearly communicate your boundaries. It allows others to know what your expectations of them are. Since we all have different boundaries, we will sometimes unintentionally cross the line with one another.

    a. Do not approach the conversation from a place of blame to avoid provoking conflict.

    b. Use the following non-violent communication to communicate your boundaries. Take a problem-solving approach.

    c. Share how the other person's actions impact you and explain how this relates to your core values. This will help them understand what your boundaries are without becoming defensive — which means they will be much more receptive to taking your message on board. For example, you could say your boss: *"One of my core values is having a healthy work-life balance so that I can spend time with my family. When you ask me to work overtime without warning, I feel that crosses a boundary and comprises my core value."*

4. Consistently maintain your boundaries

    a. When dealing with crossed boundaries, keep your core values at the forefront of your mind and refer to them during the conversation.

    b. Use a constructive approach that will lead to less conflict and greater harmony and understanding.

_____

_____

_____

_____

_____

_____

_____

_____

_____

_____

BOUNDARIES WORKSHEET – PERSONAL BOUNDARIES

INSTRUCTIONS: In the table given below, write down some of the healthy boundaries in your relationship and think of ways in which you can improve them further. In the next table, recall and write down the unhealthy boundaries to your relationship. Mention the ways in which you can replace them with healthy boundaries.

Healthy Boundaries in My Relationships	Ways to Improve Them

Unhealthy Boundaries in My Relationships	Ways to Replace Them with Healthy Ones

https://optimistminds.com/boundaries-worksheets/

Pillar: Loving

BOUNDARIES WORKSHEET – PERSONAL BOUNDARIES

INSTRUCTIONS: Personal boundaries of an individual define his/her likes and dislikes, personal beliefs, emotions, etc. in the table given below write down your personal boundaries and the way, you would tell others about these. Also, mention the ways your boundaries can be violated and your reaction in that case.

Personal Boundaries	How do I communicate these Others	How Someone Can Violate my Personal Boundaries	My Reaction When Someone Violates my Boundaries

https://optimistminds.com/boundaries-worksheets/

Week 11 & 12 Activities

YOUTH ACTIVITIES

Love Begins in Me

LESSON VOCABULARY WORDS

INSTRUCTIONS: Study the vocabulary words listed below for a good understanding of each one.

1. **Self-care:** The practice of taking action to preserve or improve one's health.
2. **Stress:** A state of mental or emotional strain.
3. **Meditation:** Continued or extended thought; reflection; contemplation.
4. **Prevention:** The act of preventing or hindering.

SELF-CARE: Self-care is anything you enjoy doing that helps make you happy and maintains your physical, mental, or emotional health.

1. Why is it important to take care of ourselves?

   _____
   _____
   _____

2. Should females/males just "*get over it*" when they are stressed?

   _____
   _____
   _____

Discussion Questions:

1. Have you ever experienced stress at home or in school?

   _____
   _____

2. Do you have a safe place and person to share your concerns and/or stressors?

   _____
   _____

Pillar: Loving

3. How much time do you dedicate to self-care?
   _____
   _____

4. List your self-care routines below:
   a. _____
   b. _____
   c. _____
   d. _____
   e. _____
   f. _____
   g. _____
   h. _____
   i. _____
   j. _____
   k. _____
   l. _____
   m. _____

Intentional Mentoring Mentee's Workbook

HOW DO I FEEL RIGHT NOW?

Pillar: Loving

Before and after participating in each activity identify how you are feeling by using the *"How Do I Feel Right Now"* Chart above.

Anchor Breathing

Anchor breathing helps you to focus your mind on one point and reduces stress. Take a deep inhale — as if you were going to blow a balloon — for four seconds. Pause and gently hold your breath for four seconds, deeply exhale through your nose for four seconds. Pause and hold the exhale for 4 seconds. Repeat 4-5 times. Anchor Breathing method also works with hands placed gently on the belly or in front of the nose.

Step Sounds

1. Imagine being on a boat, feeling calm and safe.
2. Attached to the boat is an anchor. It keeps you there, where you want to be, and happy.
3. Our bodies, like the boat, also have anchors, and they can help us focus. Our belly, our nose and mouth, and our chest and lungs can help us feel grounded.
4. With your hands on your chest, breathe in deeply.
5. Breathe out slowly.
6. Feel your ribs rise and fall.
7. As your mind wanders, gently bring it back to the anchor point.

Nature Play

Senses, often underused, such as sound, can heighten a sense of awareness and promote mindfulness. This can be especially true in an unfamiliar environment, including walking through the countryside with family.

Step Sounds

1. Pause and listen
2. What can you hear that is nearby?
3. What can you hear that is far away?
4. What is the loudest sound?
5. What is the quietest sound?
6. Can you walk without making a noise?

Meditation on the Soles of the Feet

INSTRUCTIONS:

1. If you are standing, assume a natural rather than an aggressive posture, with the soles of your feet flat on the floor. If sitting, relax with the soles of your feet flat on the floor.

2. Think about a time when something caused you to experience strong anger. Try to reconnect to that experience. Try to relive the experience that caused anger.

3. You are feeling anger, and angry thoughts may arise. Let the thoughts flow naturally without pushing them away. Stay with anger. You may have physical reactions that display anger, including an increased heart rate, increased breathing rate, and tension in the jaw, neck, and/or shoulders.

4. Shift the focus of your attention to the soles of your feet.

5. Slowly, move your toes, feel your shoes covering your feet, the texture of your socks or hose, the curve of your arch, and the heels of your feet against the back of your shoes. If you do not have shoes on, feel the floor or carpet with the soles of your feet.

6. Keep breathing naturally and focus on the soles of your feet until you feel calm.

7. Practice this exercise until you can use it wherever you are and whenever an incident occurs that may cause you to feel the urge to be verbally or physically aggressive.

8. Remember that once you are calm, you can walk away from the incident or situation with a smile on your face because you regulated your anger. Alternatively, if you need to, you can respond to the incident or situation with a calm and clear mind and without verbal threats or physical aggression.

Daily Journaling

A journal can be a fruitful way to track life's ups and downs. By capturing what went well, it is possible to identify and record the skills and talents for reuse in other areas of your life. Journaling allows people to clarify their thoughts and feelings, thereby gaining valuable self-knowledge. It's also a good problem-solving tool; oftentimes, one can hash out a problem and come up with solutions more easily on paper. Journaling about traumatic events helps one process them by fully exploring and releasing the emotions involved, and by engaging both hemispheres of the brain in the process, allowing the experience to become fully integrated within one's mind. Journaling can also help you to focus on areas of your life that you like to focus on more often, as is the case with gratitude journaling or even coincidence journaling.

EMPLOYEE OR COMMUNITY CITIZEN ACTIVITIES

Love Begins in Me

LESSON VOCABULARY WORDS

INSTRUCTIONS: Study the vocabulary words listed below for a good understanding of each one.

1. **Self-care:** The practice of taking action to preserve or improve one's health.
2. **Self-love:** is the practice of understanding, embracing, and showing compassion for yourself. It is adoration of your strengths and acceptance of your weaknesses.
3. **Stress:** A state of mental or emotional strain.
4. **Meditation:** Continued or extended thought; reflection; contemplation.
5. **Prevention:** The act of preventing or hindering.

SELF-CARE is an integral part of self-love which is the practice of being kind and compassionate towards yourself. Here are 5 ways to begin practicing self-love:

   a. *Identify your subpersonalities.* Within all of us, there are subtle and incessant voices that sabotage and paralyze us – these are the voices of our subpersonalities. Awareness is the key to overcoming the negative self-talk. To quiet these voices, practice self-compassionate mindfulness.

   b. *Identify toxic people in your life.* Learn to distance yourself (or flat out remove from your life) those who hinder your self-growth is a difficult, but necessary. A toxic person is often judgmental, manipulative, clingy, backstabbing, ruthless, aggressive, controlling, deceptive, self-pitying, and/or self-destructive.

   c. *Seek supportive community.* Supportive people encourage, uplift, and inspire us they have obtained a certain level of self-love. Because of their ability to respect themselves, they can easily respect and love others. Invite these individuals into your life and build lasting relationships with them. They can also act as accountability partners as you continue your professional and personal journey.

   d. *Make time to explore your passions.* What drives you? Fires you up? Fills you with joy and a sense of accomplishment. Sit down with these questions and ponder them deeply. Remember, passions are not static – they evolve with us. Whether painting, writing, dancing, designing, building or whatever excites you – pursue it – even if on the sidelines!

   e. *Do a digital detox (aka. stop spending so much time on social media!).* To practice self-love, we need to regularly practice digital detoxes. A digital detox involves voluntarily refusing to use any form of social media for a period of a few days to a month or more. Uninstall the apps on your phone. Go outside. Plan to do something more nourishing with your time. Journal about your progress. The benefits can often be felt within a day!

Pillar: Loving

Discussion Questions:

1. Have you ever experienced stress at home or at work?
   _____
   _____

2. Do you have toxic people in your life? If yes, describe why you say they are toxic?
   _____
   _____
   _____
   _____

3. Do you have a safe place and person to share your concerns and/or stressors?
   _____
   _____

4. How much time do you dedicate to self-care?
   _____
   _____

5. List your self-care routines below:
   a. _____
   b. _____
   c. _____
   d. _____
   e. _____
   f. _____
   g. _____
   h. _____
   i. _____
   j. _____
   k. _____

Intentional Mentoring Mentee's Workbook

DATE: _____

SELF-CARE ACTIVITIES

_____   _____
_____   _____
_____   _____

AFFIRMATION

- _____
- _____
- _____
- _____

TODAY'S MOOD

☹ 🙁 😐 🙂 😃

I'M GRATEFUL FOR:

_____

_____

_____

INSPIRATION: ....

....

....

Pillar: Loving

MY 'LOVE LETTER' TO MYSELF

The purpose of this exercise is for you to identify your many great qualities and how they benefit you. You also, will come up with ways to practice your strengths in daily life. This self-love exercise will help you to focus on your best traits, abilities, and talents. In doing so, you are on your way to becoming a more self-confident and resilient individual.

Step 1: Think about the things you love most about yourself. Focus on qualities of your personality that make you unique, strong, or lovable. For example:

♥ I am: *Honest*

♥ I am: *Brave*

♥ I am: *Creative*

Now list your positive qualities below:

♥ I am: _____

♥ I am: _____

♥ I am: _____

♥ I am: _____

♥ I am: _____

♥ I am: _____

♥ I am: _____

♥ I am: _____

Step 2: Consider the ways in which these qualities have benefited you or someone else in your life. For example:

♥ The quality of honesty has benefited me because my boss trusts me to work on important projects independently.

♥ The quality of bravery has benefited me because I got through a very painful situation in my life and became stronger because of it.

♥ The quality of creativity has benefited me because I have created artwork that I am proud to display in my home.

Now list the benefits of your positive qualities below:

♥ The quality of _____ has benefited me because: _____.

♥ The quality of _____ has benefited me because: _____.

♥ The quality of _____ has benefited me because: _____.

♥ The quality of _____ has benefited me because: _____.

♥ The quality of _____ has benefited me because: _____.

♥ The quality of _____ has benefited me because: _____.

♥ The quality of _____ has benefited me because: _____.

♥ The quality of _____ has benefited me because: _____.

Pillar: Loving

Step 3: Next come up with ways to honor these qualities in ways that are personally meaningful to you. For example:

♥ *I will remind myself that I am a good and honest person each day.*

♥ *When faced with challenges, I will remember the times I have overcome adversity in my life.*

♥ *I will continue to create because doing so makes me feel more fulfilled and content.*

Now list the ways you will honor your positive qualities below:

♥ I am:

♥ I am:

♥ I am:

♥ I am:

♥ I am:

♥ I am:

♥ I am:

♥ I am:

Now that you have completed your "letter," keep it handy and feel free to add to it when you learn more wonderful things about yourself!

https://positive.b-cdn.net/wp-content/uploads/Self-love_My-Love-Letter-to-Myself-1.pdf

SELF-CARE ROUTINES LIST

Self-Care Activities	Date Completed
1.	
2.	
3.	
4.	
5.	
6.	
7.	
8.	
9.	
10.	
11.	
12.	
13.	
14.	
15.	
16.	
17.	
18.	
19.	
20.	
21.	
22.	
23.	
24.	
25.	
26.	

Pillar: Loving

SELF-COMPASSION PAUSE. Use the following three steps during stressful encounters:

1. **Pause.** Take special notice of your breath. Notice what you feel.
2. **Use the power of touch.** Hug yourself or put your hand on your chest.
3. **Say to yourself.** "This is a difficult moment for me. I am experiencing suffering. Suffering is a part of life. I accept myself as I am."

Week 13 & 14 Activities

YOUTH ACTIVITIES

The Power of Giving

LESSON VOCABULARY WORDS

INSTRUCTIONS: Study the vocabulary words listed below for a good understanding of each one.

1. **Encourage:** To inspire with courage, spirit, or hope.
2. **Impact**: to have a direct effect.
3. **Recognition:** Formal acknowledgment.
4. **Volunteer:** A person who voluntarily undertakes a service.
5. **Giving:** To make a present.
6. **Kindness:** Courtesy, mercy, service.
7. **Community Service**: non-paying job performed by one person or a group of people for the benefit of their community or its institutions.

Pillar: Loving

Random Acts of Kindness
Journal

S S M T W T F

Date | Planned Act

be kind and grateful

What did I learn about myself?
_____
_____
_____
_____
_____

How were my random acts received?
_____
_____
_____
_____
_____

Who did I inspire from my random acts of kindness?
_____
_____
_____
_____

Notes:
_____
_____
_____
_____
_____

Intentional Mentoring Mentee's Workbook

Project Planner
COMMUNITY SERVICE

MONTH: _____

COMMUNITY SERVICE PROJECT TITLE

ANTICIPATED START DATE

ANTICIPATED DEADLINE

IDEAS

_____
_____
_____
_____
_____
_____
_____
_____
_____

to-do list

_____
_____
_____
_____
_____
_____
_____
_____
_____
_____

notes

_____
_____
_____
_____
_____
_____
_____
_____
_____
_____

JOURNAL PAGES

Pillar: Loving

EMPLOYEE OR COMMUNITY CITIZEN ACTIVITIES

Pillar: Loving

The Power of Giving

LESSON VOCABULARY WORDS

INSTRUCTIONS: Study the vocabulary words listed below for a good understanding of each one.

1. **Encourage:** To inspire with courage, spirit, or hope.
2. **Impact**: to have a direct effect.
3. **Recognition:** Formal acknowledgment.
4. **Volunteer:** A person who voluntarily undertakes a service.
5. **Giving:** To make a present.
6. **Kindness:** Courtesy, mercy, service.
7. **Community Service:** non-paying job performed by one person or a group of people for the benefit of their community or its institutions.

The following are three benefits of Community Service:

   a. **Curbs biases and judgments**. Community service opens you to a door of multi-cultural diversity. It's a chance to forget about the judgments, biases, and stigma you may have. Open your mind, and show that despite the differences, everyone deserves a better life and equal opportunities.

INCREASES SELF-EFFICACY. Self-efficacy is a person's belief in their ability to succeed in a particular situation. It allows people to gauge their own competence and build their confidence. It inspires them to continuously grow and become more efficient when dealing with day-to-day decision-making.

Random Acts of Kindness
Journal

be kind and grateful

S M T W T F S

DATE | PLANNED ACT

What did I learn about myself?

How were my random acts received?

Who did I inspire from my random acts of kindness?

Notes:

Pillar: Loving

Project Planner
COMMUNITY SERVICE

MONTH: _____

COMMUNITY SERVICE PROJECT TITLE

ANTICIPATED START DATE

ANTICIPATED DEADLINE

IDEAS

_____
_____
_____
_____
_____
_____
_____
_____

to-do list

_____
_____
_____
_____
_____
_____
_____
_____
_____

notes

_____
_____
_____
_____
_____
_____
_____
_____
_____

JOURNAL PAGES

Pillar: Loving

Week 15 & 16 Activities

YOUTH ACTIVITIES

Pillar: Loving

The Community of Love

LESSON VOCABULARY WORDS

INSTRUCTIONS: Study the vocabulary words listed below for a good understanding of each one.

1. **Community:** A group of people living in the same place or having a particular characteristic in common. a feeling of fellowship with others, as a result of sharing common attitudes, interests, and goals.

2. **Vision:** The ability to think about or plan the future with imagination or wisdom.

3. **Strength:** A good or beneficial quality or attribute of a person or thing.

Discussion Questions:

1. Do you think it's important for you to have a community?

   _____
   _____
   _____

2. Have you ever heard the phrase, "it takes a village?" Who did you hear it from? How was it used? What does it mean to you?

   _____
   _____
   _____

3. Who makes up your community?

   _____
   _____
   _____

4. What led you to the Mentoring Program? Is this now a part of your community?

   _____
   _____
   _____

Building a Community Bingo Questionnaire

INSTRUCTIONS: Answer the following questions in preparation for playing the Bingo Game and find others who match your answers.

1. Who is your hero? _____
2. I have a puppy and his/her name is? _____
3. What is your biggest fear? _____
4. What is your favorite family vacation? _____
5. My favorite hiding or quiet space is? _____
6. What makes you angry? _____
7. What motivates you to work hard? _____
8. What is your favorite subject in school? _____
9. What is your biggest complaint about school or home? _____
10. What is your proudest accomplishment? _____
11. What do you do best? _____
12. What is your favorite book to read? _____
13. What makes you laugh? _____
14. What was the last movie you went to see? What did you think? ____
15. What did you want to do when you grow up? _____
16. Have you ever had a nickname? What is it? _____
17. Do you like or dislike surprises? Why or why not? _____
18. What's your favorite zoo animal? _____
19. Who is your favorite comic strip character? _____
20. What's your favorite movie? _____
21. Who is your favorite Disney character? _____
22. Are you the oldest, middle, or youngest child in your family? ___
23. I love video games and I am really good at: _____
24. My favorite movie is: _____

Building a Community
BINGO

B	I	N	G	O
11	9	2	16	5
4	15	6	12	21
24	18	FREE	8	14
7	20	10	13	22
1	17	23	19	3

EMPLOYEE OR COMMUNITY CITIZEN ACTIVITIES

Pillar: Loving

The Community of Love

LESSON VOCABULARY WORDS

INSTRUCTIONS: Study the vocabulary words listed below for a good understanding of each one.

1. **Community:** A group of people living in the same place or having a particular characteristic in common. a feeling of fellowship with others, as a result of sharing common attitudes, interests, and goals.

2. **Vision:** The ability to think about or plan the future with imagination or wisdom.

3. **Strength:** A good or beneficial quality or attribute of a person or thing.

Discussion Questions:

1. Do you think it's important for you to have a community?
   _____
   _____
   _____

2. Have you ever heard the phrase, "it takes a village?" Who did you hear it from? How was it used? What does it mean to you?
   _____
   _____
   _____

3. Who makes up your community?
   _____
   _____
   _____

4. What led you to the Mentoring Program? Is this now a part of your community?
   _____
   _____
   _____

WHO IS YOUR SUPPORTIVE COMMUNITY?

One of the most important aspects of healthy human functioning is having a strong, reliable support system. They say it takes a village to raise a child, but a village is important even in adulthood. For some, their support system does in fact start in childhood. They have parents, grandparents, siblings, teachers, teammates that all help them find their place in life, give them advice when things become challenging, teach them right from wrong. But for others, building their tribe is a much more intentional process in adulthood. Have participants think about their supportive community, who they are and what makes them a part of their supportive community. Have the Participants share something about at least 2 of the people on their list.

Members of Supportive Community	What's their role and what makes them a part of your community?
1.	
2.	
3.	
4.	
5.	

Accountability Partner Tracker

ACCOUNTABILITY PARTNER'S NAME:	
	Add your goal to the following worksheet, then use the Accountability Tracker to ensure your goals/objectives are being met.
GOAL	
ACTION STEP	
ACTION STEP	
ACTION STEP	
GOAL	
ACTION STEP	
ACTION STEP	
ACTION STEP	
GOAL	
ACTION STEP	
ACTION STEP	
ACTION STEP	
GOAL	
ACTION STEP	
ACTION STEP	
ACTION STEP	

PILLAR: LEARNING

PILLAR: LEARNING

Merriam-Webster dictionary defines learning as the acquisition of knowledge or skills through experience, study, or by being taught. In psychology, learning is defined as the relatively permanent change in behavior because of an experience. I sat in this space writing and rewriting this pillar concerned that the information being disseminated will be relevant, usable, and inspiring. So, I went back to the drawing board to determine why I chose education as a career. Like many others, I chose a career in education to help mold the minds and lives of the next generation. To help them navigate their educational career with the support, opportunities, and information that does more than just have students rotely memorize the information and regurgitated on a test, term paper, and/or during a class discussion. I wanted the lessons I taught to be seen as the living and exciting aspects of life, development, and growth they truly are. If I am being truthful, that is part of my motivation that energized and empowered me to begin the Mentoring Project. Take a minute and truly consider why you are considering starting a mentoring program and what you hope the mentor and mentee will take away from the experience. Initially, I was going to inundate you with the statistical data that proves the cultural, economic, and financial disparities that are woven into the fabric of America. Instead, I thought about the benefits of this pillar, as a level in the foundation both the mentor and mentee are building and securing, will be the place in which they spring forth to live the life of their choosing. So many times, people are judged by their last poor choice, bad act, circumstance surrounding their birth, and/or the communities they live in. I purposefully left out their race because that is a horse of a different color and is something that cannot be changed or taught. Everyone must come into the realization of self that is spoken about in the pillar on LIVING.

LEARNING is a choice, a conscious decision that is intentionally acted upon. It isn't something that happens by accident or unwillingly. Learning, if done correctly and received intentionally, has the power to change the person's perspective, viewpoint of themselves and their view of the world around them. It also influences how they allow the world to impact them and how they impact the world around them. I mentioned this before and find it relevant here as well. Doctor Phil said, "*…you cannot choose the behavior without also choosing the circumstance.*" That is also true in education. You cannot choose to be present and participate in the learning as it takes place and not receive the information shared to impact your life in some way, shape, or form. Nor can you walk away from the responsibility you now have to what you have learned. Which shines a light on what Maya Angelou said, "*…when you know better, do better.*" I know you are wondering why I ventured away from the style and playbook of the other pillars. The truth of the matter is this is one of the most important pillars the mentor will share with and teach to the mentee. The mentor must allow him/herself to learn the pillars on LIVING and LOVING to ensure they present the lesson on LEARNING in a way that encourages, empowers, and enables the mentee to accept responsibility for the information they receive and the courage to activate it in their life. In a way that gives them permission to envision a life outside of the confines of their community, home, and/or societal limitations.

Let's revisit the definition of learning. The key components of the definition are (1) acquisition, (2) knowledge, (3) skills, and (4) experience. Follow me here because I am going somewhere. Acquisition is defined as an asset or object bought or obtained; the learning or developing of a skill, habit, or quality. Knowledge is the facts, information, and skills gained by a person through experience or education; and awareness or familiarity gained by experience of a fact or situation. Skill is the ability to do something well or with expertise, the ability to use one's knowledge effectively and readily. An experience is the process of doing and seeing things and of having things happen to you, an encounter, event, or occurrence. Each of the words defined above are components of learning and are relative only to the individual who is experiencing the episode of learning that is occurring at that moment. Learning does not happen without each aspect that is previously mentioned happening simultaneously. All while empowering and enabling the learner to show up and take part in their own life to activate, cultivate, and give themselves permission to use the information in the season of life, it is most needed and effective.

LEARNING only happens when we see the value in acquiring or getting the information for internal or external use. Sometimes the information is only valuable to you because of your own personal values and the accomplishments you desire for your life. The value is determined based upon how the information can be used and how the learner will use it to change their perspectives, attitude, and altitude. I was watching a movie and there was a scene where the character was holding on for dear life because they did not know how far down the ground was beneath their feet. Another character came along to help them and didn't stop quick enough and ended up falling into the limitless and smoke covered bottom. Their landing resounded with a loud thud and when they stood up, their nose was at the same level as the other characters' waist. Once the character realized the floor was closer than they initially thought, they released what they were holding onto and dropped to the floor. The lack of information left character #1 uncertain and afraid to act or even move. However, once the

Pillar: Learning

character had the information they initially lacked, they received it and acted upon it. In that moment, character #1 had the freedom to make a decision that changed their perspective and made the decision that was the right one for them at that moment.

According to *4 Types of Learning Styles*, there are four learning styles: visual, auditory, reading and writing, and kinesthetic.

1. Visual learners are better able to retain information when it is presented to them in a graphic depiction.
2. Auditory learners prefer listening to information that is being presented vocally.
3. Reading and writing learners focus on the written word, reading and writing, and other text-heavy resources.
4. Kinesthetic learners are hands-on thrive when engaging all their senses during coursework and/or learning opportunities.

For the mentee to benefit and find value in this pillar, the mentor must identify their unique learning style and present the information in a manner that catches the mentee's attention. Do not assume your mentee learns in the same way you do. Ask! Pay attention to him/her and see how he/she responds to the information. It will give you the insight you need to determine their particular learning style.

In mentoring, LEARNING is the component or the result that happens from each mentor-mentee interaction. Do not leave these experiences to chance. Plan them out with your mentee's style of learning and personal interests in mind. For the purposes of this book, LEARNING comprises the various ways information can be shared and/or introduced to the mentee during group sessions and/or individual mentor-mentee interactions. I have found that using open discussion after a lesson or an opportunity to experience the information learned in real time is more effective than just listening. For example, if the lesson is being taught on life skills, the mentor can offer real-life scenarios where the mentee applies the information, he/she has learned. This will provide the mentee with a reference point that helps them process and remember the information. Another example is if the lesson is about discipline and organization. The mentor can take their mentee to a ballet or interpretive dance program, and afterwards have a question-and-answer session with the dancers. During the session, the mentor and mentee can ask questions about what they did to reach their current level of success and/or how they've organized their lives to become successful dancers. The same scenario can be used with any profession. Once they finish the question-and-answer session, ask the mentees what they learned and to give an example of how they can incorporate the learned life lessons into their everyday life!

As mentioned before, learning is an experience and it presents itself differently based upon who is sharing or teaching the information, and who receives, interprets, and uses the information. Not to mention how they decide to activate or use the information. The mentor may look at the information being shared as common-sense information, while the mentee is receiving new information that expands their awareness and their view of themselves, their community, and even the world. Which affords the mentor a rare yet rewarding opportunity to experience the occurrence through the wonderment and excitement as the mentee experiences it. It changes them both in that moment. The mentor develops a new point of reference that teaches him/her how to view, process, and/or share information going forward. The mentor realizes another aspect of who they are and how they can affect change in the world, one mentee at a time. The mentee receives the information and sees themselves in a larger picture or on a world stage. Whereas previously, they could not see themselves outside of the confines of their community and/or their cultural and/or economic limitations. They have the chance to envision a life that is limitless. Regardless of the setting, the opportunity to learn, grow, and evolve helps both the mentor and the mentee to develop and experience life differently going forward. During the mentor-mentee interactions, they both develop the role each will play in the other person's life, and in what their mentoring relationship needs to look like for them to continue growing forward. What most people cannot recognize or realize is that every experience and/or information received changes who each of them are especially when the impact of the experience/information has left an indelible mark on their heart and/or mind. A fact of life that cannot be disputed in any way is that while the mentor and mentee have breath in their body, they will be in a constant state of learning.

GUIDANCE

Throughout the history of mankind, it has become apparent that humans learn better when they take part in peer-to-peer learning opportunities. Mentoring is another aspect of peer-to-peer learning that presents the mentee with the modeling of behavior that leads or guides them to experiencing successful outcomes and first-hand experiences with identifying the skills and tools exemplified in leaders. Mentoring has become a universal opportunity to build a sense of self, improve personal and/or professional development, create a supportive learning environment, open up avenues for exposure to opportunities and possibilities previously unknown to them, and an emotional support system for both the mentor and mentee during critical moments in each of their lives. Which is why schools, corporations, and organizations have created mentoring programs where leadership mentor's frontline and subordinate employees, teachers and/or community leaders mentor students/youth, and youth centers and/or youth organizations create programming where mentoring occurs in group settings. In schools, it has become even more effective when mentees are paired with educators who share their same ethnic and cultural beliefs. In corporations and/or organizations, it has become even more effective when mentees are paired with executive level personnel or community leaders who have attained the level of success they desire, but don't have access to.

In every instance, mentees, whether students in an educational setting, adults/youth in a community setting, or adults in the workplace, benefit from the guidance mentoring offers to better understand their pathway when navigating life, and when gaining knowledge. This is an essential ingredient in their development of their sense of self and when moving towards their purpose, they plan their long-term personal and/or professional goals. The trust relationship that is built between the mentor and mentee empowers the mentee to create a ripple effect, where they become a mentor to those coming up behind him/her. They take what they have learned and experienced as a mentee to create a relationship with a mentee that opens the mentee up to a whole new world of opportunities and possibilities.

Alan Bruce said, *"Even learning include strong elements of guidance... these elements of guidance are to enable the mentee to reflect, consider options, and in the end make choices based on the information... Guidance can point out the consequences of choices made by the mentee..."* All of which are necessary for the mentee to grow and mature while developing the confidence that the choices/decisions they face may be the right one for them to make. While actively considering if it is the right choice/decision for him/her to make during this time in their life. This is the case regardless if the mentee is a youth or an employee in a Fortune 500 company. Learning involves the introduction and retention of information that opens his/her eyes to see a world that is more accessible to them and has the potential of opening doors they may have never known were available to them. Doors that offer him/her entrance, access and/or the lenses to see a world outside of the confines of the one they have become comfortable and content living within.

According to *The Master's Voice: Learning Through Mentoring*, "*Mentoring plays a valuable role in imparting skills, attitudes, and experience-based lessons to develop relationships of trust and interactive communication in a paradigm of shared goals. It is a neutral space… that plays a vital role in developing the critical judgement, analytical skills and decision-making skills necessary for continued growth and development throughout the various phases of life.*" As the mentees have new experiences and take in more information, he/she understands and recognizes the choices they make today have the power to open or lock doors to the future currently available to him/her.

In every instance in my life, I have found anything worth having is worth working for, being committed to, and organizing my life to make it a reality. There is no greater feeling in the world than attaining your goals and respecting the hard work you put into it. That feeling of satisfaction can only be felt/experienced. Attempting to express those feelings in words does not do it justice! Which shines a light on the need for mentoring programs in schools, corporations and/or organizations and the benefits enjoyed by both the mentor and mentee.

Week 17 & 18 Activities

YOUTH ACTIVITIES

Pillar: Learning

Career Vs. Job

LESSON VOCABULARY WORDS

INSTRUCTIONS: Review vocabulary words listed below with the participants to ensure they have a good understanding of each before starting any of the activities.

1. **Career**: One or more jobs in the same area of interest.
2. **Job**: Work that one does for pay.
3. **Salary:** A fixed amount of pay for a certain period.
4. **Wages:** A fixed amount of money paid for each hour worked.
5. **Communication:** the imparting or exchanging of information or news.
6. **Guidance:** the act or process of guiding; advice on vocational or educational goals.

Discussion Questions:

1. Have you ever considered how Important is it to have a plan for your life?

   _____
   _____

2. Do you believe education alone helps people move up in their careers?

   _____
   _____

List of Careers and Jobs

Dentist	Cashier
Registered Nurse	Cook
Pharmacist	Automotive Technician
Information Security Analyst	Bartender
Software Developer	Office Assistant
Lawyer	Janitor
Physician	Assembly Line Technician
Veterinarian	Mailroom Clerk
Anesthesiologists	Front Desk Attendant
Occupational Therapist	Receptionist

Career vs. Job
How They're Different and Why It Matters

What is the difference between a career and job? Though these terms are often used to describe the same thing, they do have different meanings. The main purpose for obtaining a job is to earn money. With a job, people have a short-term goal of doing the work at the job. Most plan to be at a job for a year or two. They don't plan on doing the same job for life. They plan to be at a job until they decide on a career or start a career. Also, most jobs don't require specialized skills, training, or a higher education. Though a job can be full-time, many jobs are part-time, and temporary work. When we are younger, we often have a job to earn some money or gain some work experience before starting our career. What is a career? A career is a profession.

---

1. What is often the main purpose of a job? _____

True or False

2. _____ People typically plan to have the same job for the long-term.

3. _____ Most people have a job until they decide or start a career.

4. _____ Most jobs don't require specialized skills, training, or higher education.

It is an occupation in a specific field of work. Some examples of careers are a carpenter, nurse, fire fighter, or a lawyer. With a career, we specialize in a field of work. We plan to stay working in a selected career for the long-term. With a career, the person plans to grow and develop their skills and advance in their field or profession. Also, careers often require obtaining specialized training, a set of skills, and/or a higher education. Unlike a job, motivation for a career is not mainly money. Instead, we are often motivated to obtain a certain career because of the desire for personal satisfaction, advancement, and eventually higher earning ability. What are the benefits of a job? Though the main motivation for obtaining a job is often money, there are many other benefits to having a job. A job gives you the opportunity to learn and improve key soft skills. Soft skills are those behaviors and social skills used in all workplaces. Some examples of key soft skills are teamwork, communication, dependability, and a

Directions: Answer each question.

1. What is a career?

2. Are careers long-term or short-term?

3. What do careers often require?

4. What are often the motivations to obtain a career?

Pillar: Learning

strong work- ethic. Developing your soft skills improves your future job and career opportunities. When employers are looking for job candidates, they desire those candidates who possess a set of strong soft skills. Hence, when you have a job, it is important to take it seriously. Remember, it is not just a job, but an opportunity. You will learn valuable soft skills that will make you highly desired by employers. Also, a job can be a good testing ground to see if you like a certain type of work or career. You never know, because what might have begun as a job can turn into a great career. What are the benefits of a career?

Fill-in the blanks with the best word from the right-side.

1. A job gives you an opportunity to develop the _____.

2. Soft skills are those _____ and social skills used in the workplace.

3. Examples of key soft skills are communication, dependability, and _____.

4. _____ desire job candidate with a set of strong soft skills.

The benefits of choosing a career far outweigh the benefits of having a job. Choosing a career increases your job security, especially if you select a career that is in high demand.

Because careers take a unique set of skills and/or education, a career tends to be more stable than a job. Careers cannot be easily replaced by machines, replaced by others, or impacted by social-economic changes. You also have a higher earning ability and a greater opportunity for advancement with a career. Also, those who have careers experience greater job satisfaction because they are doing what they like. They also feel a sense of purpose and accomplishment. Though a career takes planning, commitment, and sacrifice, it is well worth the effort. In fact, having a rewarding future will typically depend upon having a career.

True or False

1. _____ A job has more benefits than a career.

2. _____ Careers have more job security than a job.

3. _____ With a career, you will have a higher earning ability.

4. _____ A career gives you greater job satisfaction and purpose.

Teamwork ♦ Behaviors ♦ Employers ♦ Soft Skills

Career vs. a Job

Identify How They Are Different

• Short-term pursuit Long-term pursuit • Earning money is the main motivation Motivated by personal satisfaction and • Often done before starting a career • Higher earning potential • Nurse • Hostess at a restaurant • Carpenter	• A profession • Often requires a set of skills, education, or specialized training • Takes planning and commitment • Often doesn't require unique skills or education • Has more job security • Supports learning and developing soft skills • Police officer • Cashier

Directions: Place the terms from above in the correct box below.

A Job =	A Career =

Pillar: Learning

Vocabulary Practice

Career vs. a Job

Career	Job
Soft skills	Profession
Employer	Job security
Part-time	Advancement

Directions: Select the best term for each sentence.

1. A/An _____ is the company that employs or puts a person to work.

2. A/An _____ is a profession or occupation in a specific field of work that requires a set of skills.

3. _____ is when a job is more secure and is unlikely to be dismissed.

4. A/An _____ is work that is primarily motivated by earning money and is usually short-term.

5. A/An _____ job position is when a person works only part of the day or week.

6. A/An _____ is the promotion of a person at work to a higher position.

7. A/An _____ is considered a career or occupation in a specific field of work.

EMPLOYEE OR COMMUNITY CITIZEN ACTIVITIES

Pillar: Learning

Career Vs. Job

LESSON VOCABULARY WORDS

INSTRUCTIONS: Review vocabulary words listed below with the participants to ensure they have a good understanding of each before starting any of the activities.

1. **Career**: One or more jobs in the same area of interest.
2. **Job**: Work that one does for pay.
3. **Salary:** A fixed amount of pay for a certain period.
4. **Wages:** A fixed amount of money paid for each hour worked.
5. **Communication:** the imparting or exchanging of information or news.
6. **Guidance:** the act or process of guiding; advice on vocational or educational goals.

Discussion Questions:

1. Have you ever considered how Important is it to have a plan for your life?

   _____
   _____
   _____

2. Do you believe education alone helps people move up in their careers?

   _____
   _____
   _____

List of Careers and Jobs

Dentist	Cashier
Registered Nurse	Cook
Pharmacist	Automotive Technician
Information Security Analyst	Bartender
Software Developer	Office Assistant
Lawyer	Janitor
Physician	Assembly Line Technician
Veterinarian	Mailroom Clerk
Anesthesiologists	Front Desk Attendant
Occupational Therapist	Receptionist

Week 19 & 20 Activities

YOUTH ACTIVITIES

Social Media and Digital Responsibility

LESSON VOCABULARY WORDS

INSTRUCTIONS: Study the vocabulary words listed below for a good understanding of each one.

1. **Social Media:** Websites and applications that enable users to create and share content or to participate in social networking.

2. **Social networking:** The use of dedicated websites and applications to interact with other users, or to find people with similar interests to oneself.

3. **Viral:** An image or video that becomes popular through a viral process of internet sharing.

4. **Cyber Bullying:** A form of bullying or harassment using electronic means. Also known as online bullying.

5. **Digital footprint:** A trail of data you create while using the internet. It includes sites you visit, what you share, where you share, and links you click.

ONLINE SAFETY TIPS

1. Don't give out personal information online (i.e. home address, school name, phone number, etc.)
2. Never send pictures of you or your family to strangers.
3. Keep your passwords private except from parents.
4. Don't download anything without your parent/guardian's permission.
5. Tell an adult if you receive a mean, vulgar and/or strange message.
6. Don't live your life online by oversharing.

Discussion Questions: Answer the following questions in preparation of the group discussion.

1. Do you have a social media account or page? Yes or No. (Circle your answer.)
2. What do you use your social media for?

_____
_____
_____
_____
_____

Pillar: Learning

3. What is Cyberbullying?

   _____
   _____
   _____

4. Can I be refused entrance into a university or college because of my online activities?

   _____
   _____
   _____

5. Have you ever seen someone post something that wasn't nice on social media?

   _____
   _____
   _____

REFLECTION: Cyberbullying can ruin lives, create scenario where it impacts another person's mental and emotional health and could lead to suicidal thoughts and/or suicide. In some cases, the person who is the bully is charged with a crime and becomes a felon. I encourage you to post positive and encouraging memes, pictures, and quotes.

EMPLOYEE OR COMMUNITY CITIZEN ACTIVITIES

Pillar: Learning

Social Media and Digital Responsibility

LESSON VOCABULARY WORDS

INSTRUCTIONS: Study the vocabulary words listed below for a good understanding of each one.

1. **Social Media:** Websites and applications that enable users to create and share content or to participate in social networking.

2. **Social networking:** The use of dedicated websites and applications to interact with other users, or to find people with similar interests to oneself.

3. **Viral:** An image or video that becomes popular through a viral process of internet sharing.

4. **Cyber Bullying:** A form of bullying or harassment using electronic means. Also known as online bullying.

5. **Digital footprint:** A trail of data you create while using the internet. It includes sites you visit, what you share, where you share, and links you click.

ONLINE SAFETY TIPS

1. Have security settings are set to a standard you are happy with to ensure only people you want to see your business gets access to it.

2. Delete any posts that you have put up in the past that do not represent who you are. It will make it difficult to find the post in the future.

3. If someone posts a piece of content that you are not happy with and tagged you in the post, un-tag yourself from the post and/or report it.

4. Delete or deactivate any unwanted or unused accounts.

5. Regularly log out of all your online profiles. Including your social media accounts.

6. Use your preferred search engine and search for yourself. See what comes up and determine if any of the information is inappropriate or unwanted and go about removing it.

Discussion Questions:

1. How are digital footprints are formed?

   _____

   _____

2. How should you be aware of and manage your digital footprint?

   _____

   _____

3. How can your online reputation be threatened and how should you defend it?

   _____
   _____
   _____

4. Have you seen a fighting video, some unkind tweets, a personal and private image, or video online? What happened?

   _____
   _____
   _____

5. How can we remain respectful and responsible online?

   _____
   _____
   _____

6. How would they feel if someone posted something about you online that was not true?

   _____
   _____
   _____

7. How would you feel if a mistake/poor decision you made became the trending story on social media?

   _____
   _____
   _____

8. How can a bad online reputation impact your everyday life and/or career?

   _____
   _____
   _____

Activity 1: Poster/Pamphlet Activity:

Create a poster or pamphlet that provides information on how someone can protect their online reputation. Come up with strategies on how best to defend an online reputation against attacks.

Pillar: Learning

Activity 2: Answer the questions.

1. What percentage of employers will use search engines to research people before offering them a position with their company? _____

2. What is at risk when a negative light or posts are found about you online? _____

3. Should you NOT be concerned about what you post? Yes or No (Circle your answer.)

REFLECTION: Digital footprints yield information about you. Your online reputation is how that information is interpreted by others to form an opinion of you as a person. Your online reputation can impact and affect relationships and potential jobs, and you may not even be aware of the negative impact it is having on your life and/or career.

Week 21 & 22 Activities

YOUTH ACTIVITIES

Organization is Key

LESSON VOCABULARY WORDS

INSTRUCTIONS: Study the vocabulary words listed below for a good understanding of each one.

1. **Organized:** Arranged systematically, especially on a large scale.
2. **Productivity:** The effectiveness of productive effort; the state or quality of producing something.
3. **Tasks:** A piece of work to be done or undertaken.
4. **Goals:** The object of a person's ambition or effort; an aim or desired result.
5. **Decluttering:** Remove unnecessary items from an untidy or overcrowded place.

TIPS TO BE MORE ORGANIZED:

1. **Break tasks into chunks.** Complete 20-minute tasks to become more organized or to complete household chores.
2. **Make a checklist and to-do lists to remain focused and on the task.** There's a sense of accomplishments when you can mark items off your list.
3. **Learn time-management skills.** It will help complete tasks and/or homework assignments on time.
4. **Establish daily routines.** Create a regular schedule so everyone knows what to expect and when tasks are to be completed.
5. **Help youth to think ahead.** Before bed have youth review the plans for the next day. It makes it easier to handle unexpected changes.

Discussion Question:

1. Do you consider yourself organized? Why or why not?

   _____
   _____
   _____

2. What is clutter?

   _____
   _____
   _____

Pillar: Learning

3. Does clutter affect your work environment at school and/or home?

   _____
   _____
   _____

HOW IMPORTANT IS BEING ORGANIZED WORKSHEET

Rate each concept from 1-5 (1 being least important 5 being most important) to determine how important being organized is in the situation.

1) Having company over for the weekend   _____

2) Having a stressful moment and cannot find anything you need   _____

3) Writing things down as they come to your mind   _____

4) You have chores to do at home   _____

5) You have little kids looking up to you and following everything you do   _____

6) Running late for a meeting   _____

7) Donating some items to charity or a homeless shelter   _____

WRITING PROMPT TOPIC: How can I practice being more organized in my daily life?

EMPLOYEE OR COMMUNITY CITIZEN ACTIVITIES

Organization is Key

LESSON VOCABULARY WORDS

INSTRUCTIONS: Study the vocabulary words listed below for a good understanding of each one.

1. **Organized:** Arranged systematically, especially on a large scale.
2. **Productivity:** The effectiveness of productive effort; the state or quality of producing something.
3. **Tasks:** A piece of work to be done or undertaken.
4. **Goals:** The object of a person's ambition or effort; an aim or desired result.
5. **Decluttering:** Remove unnecessary items from an untidy or overcrowded place.

REASONS FOR BEING ORGANIZED:

1. Being organized Reduces Stress.
2. Getting organized boosts your self-confidence.
3. Getting organized makes you more productive.
4. Being organized enhances creativity.
5. Getting organized enables you to adapt and become flexible.
6. Being organized helps you to be a good role model.
7. Getting organized improves our relationships.

TIPS TO BE MORE ORGANIZED:

1. **Break tasks into chunks.** Complete 20-minute tasks to become more organized or to complete household chores.
2. **Make a checklist and to-do lists to remain focused and on the task.** There's a sense of accomplishments when you can mark items off your list.
3. **Learn time-management skills.** It will help complete tasks and/or homework assignments on time.
4. **Establish daily routines.** Create a regular schedule so everyone knows what to expect and when tasks are to be completed.
5. **Help youth to think ahead.** Before bed have youth review the plans for the next day. It makes it easier to handle unexpected changes.

Pillar: Learning

Discussion Question:

1. Do you consider yourself organized? Why or why not?

   _____
   _____
   _____

2. What is clutter?

   _____
   _____
   _____

3. Does clutter negatively impact your work environment at school, work and/or home?

   _____
   _____
   _____

HOW IMPORTANT IS BEING ORGANIZED WORKSHEET

Rate each concept from 1-5 (1 being least important 5 being most important) to determine how important being organized is in the situation.

1) Having co-workers over for a dinner party, watch the Super Bowl or to hang out. _____

2) Having a stressful moment and cannot find anything you need. _____

3) Writing things down as they come to your mind. _____

4) You are supervising other employees and you assign their daily duties. _____

5) Running late for a meeting and don't have a good reason why. _____

6) Donating some items to charity or a homeless shelter. _____

TO DO CHECKLIST

TO DO LIST

S M T W T F S

DATES: _____

TODAY'S GOALS

REMINDER & NOTES

Week 23 & 24 Activities

YOUTH ACTIVITIES

Pillar: Learning

Health and Well-being

LESSON VOCABULARY WORDS

INSTRUCTIONS: Study the vocabulary words listed below for a good understanding of each one.

1. **Health:** The general condition of the body and mind.
2. **Healthy:** Free from infirmity or disease.
3. **Lifestyle:** A manner of living that reflects one's values and attitudes.
4. **Well-being:** The state of being comfortable, healthy, or happy.
5. **Physical Activity:** Any bodily movement that uses energy.
6. **Exercise**: Planned, structured, and purposeful physical activity.

WELLNESS WORKSHEET

1. Do you consider yourself to be healthy? Yes or No (Circle your answer.)

2. Define the Wellbeing in your own words.

   _____
   _____
   _____
   _____
   _____

3. Provide examples of individuals whose health and well-being play a huge role in how successful they are. (i.e., Simone Biles, James Harden, Stephen Curry, and JJ Wyatt).

   _____
   _____
   _____
   _____
   _____
   _____
   _____

4. "What steps can you take to make sure you are taking ownership of your health and not letting anyone disrupt your daily well-being?"

   _____
   _____
   _____
   _____
   _____
   _____

JOURNAL PAGES

Pillar: Learning

EMPLOYEE OR COMMUNITY CITIZEN ACTIVITIES

Pillar: Learning

Health and Well-Being

LESSON VOCABULARY WORDS

INSTRUCTIONS: Study the vocabulary words listed below for a good understanding of each one.

1. **Health:** The general condition of the body and mind.
2. **Healthy:** Free from infirmity or disease.
3. **Lifestyle:** A manner of living that reflects one's values and attitudes.
4. **Well-being:** The state of being comfortable, healthy, or happy.
5. **Physical Activity:** Any bodily movement that uses energy.
6. **Exercise**: Planned, structured, and purposeful physical activity.

HEALTH & WELLNESS: When talking about achieving health and wellness, it is often only referred to becoming physically healthy by getting more exercise and eating healthier. But physical wellness is only one dimension of being a healthy person. To be truly healthy, consider all the other elements of health and wellness. Having a healthy, satisfying life happens when all the elements interact seamlessly. (https://wellness411center.com/)

Activity: After watching the video clip, create a plan of action to implement health and well-being in your daily life. (https://www.healthierwork.act.gov.au/wp-content/uploads/2015/01/HW_Action_Plan_template.pdf)

10 SIMPLE WAYS TO IMPROVE YOUR HEALTH:

1. Enjoy de-stressing	Experts recommend regular exercise, meditation and breathing techniques to reduce stress.
2. Get to bed earlier.	Set a regular sleep and wake schedule and stick to it — even on days off. Going to bed even 15 minutes earlier every night could help.
3. Check your posture and ergonomics.	Take a moment to think about your posture. Then straighten up your back, tuck in your stomach and put your feet flat on the floor with your legs uncrossed. You'll feel more relaxed right away.
4. Make a few dietary substitutions.	Munch on a carrot instead of a cookie. They're rich in fiber and contain lots of water, so they'll leave you full and satisfied without a lot of calories and fat.
5. Exercise regularly.	The next time you're going to a higher floor, bypass the elevator and climb the stairs instead. Take a few minutes to stretch out before and after you exercise.

TO DO CHECKLIST

TO DO LIST

_____
_____
_____
_____
_____
_____
_____
_____
_____
_____
_____
_____
_____

S   M   T   W   T   F   S

DATES: _____

TODAY'S GOALS

_____
_____
_____
_____
_____

REMINDER & NOTES

_____
_____
_____
_____
_____
_____
_____

HEALTHY HABITS JOURNAL
(WRITE DOWN THE THINGS YOU ARE DOING TO SUPPORT A HEALTHY LIFESTYLE.)

PILLAR:
LAUGHING

PILLAR: LAUGHING

Throughout life, many have been told not to take themselves too seriously. To enjoy life and to laugh more. In the previous chapters, the mentee has learned invaluable lessons, grown into who they are meant to be in this season of their life, learned the importance of giving themselves the gift of love and how to share it with others, and they have learned that their future is bright with opportunities and possibilities. All of which is necessary! Now it is time to learn how to LAUGH! Ella Wheeler Wilcox wrote, *"Laugh, and the world laughs with you; weep, and you weep alone."* In her musings, it became clear she implied that cheerful people draw cheerful people to them. She encourages people to keep their sense of humor! In this chapter, the mentee will build upon what they have learned and LAUGH!

THE IMPORTANCE OF LAUGHTER/LAUGHING

Wow, considering how to present this chapter on laughter, I came across the following *"laughter is the language of the soul,"* - Pablo Neruda. It sets the tone and direction I will use to describe the different uses for laughter and its healing properties. All of which speak to its necessity in our lives. Robert Provine says, "*...laughter is specifically a social structure, something that connects humans with one another in a profound way.*" In his study, he found people are 30% more likely to laugh in a social setting that warrants it than when alone with humor dash inducing media. Which supports his previous statement that humans are more likely to laugh with friends than when experiencing some comedic event alone.

There are many ways in which people resort to laughter: contagious laughter, nervous laughter, and canned laughter. If you think about it, 90% of our laughter has nothing to do with responding to the joke someone told, but for various other reasons. The following are three different types of laughter and the reasons why we may use them.

CONTAGIOUS LAUGHTER: Think about the last time you were with friends or at a family gathering and someone tells a joke. A joke that isn't funny at all, but the person telling the joke laughs to the point of tears. Their laughter causes others to laugh and then you find yourself laughing. Laughing more because everyone else is laughing and not because the joke was funny. Which supports the belief that humans have laughed detectors. His belief was based on providing an explanation to why people automatically respond to laughter with laughter.

NERVOUS LAUGHTER: Nervous laughter is used to protect a person's dignity and/or to maintain control of a situation. However, a small giggle or laugh can easily turn into uncontrollable laughter without warning. Nervous laughter is usually a person's subconscious attempt to reduce stress in an attempt to calm down, but in most cases, it does the complete opposite. It usually heightens the uncomfortableness of the situation.

CANNED LAUGHTER: Canned laughter is genuine laughter that is taken completely out of context and place. Canned laughter is usually used to influence or cause an audience to find humor in the comedic material being shared or in response to it. This type of laughter is designed with contagious laughter in mind and was introduced in television in the 1950s.

CRUEL LAUGHTER: Cruel laughter is laughter that is used at another person's expense. It is considered as being cruel and insensitive. Most people who participate in cruel laughter did not initially set out to do so. Someone falls and hurts himself/herself, and an onlooker laughs. Other witnesses look at him/her, thinking their laughter is inappropriate. The person laughing realizes its inappropriateness and tries to stop laughing, and sometimes they are successful but not always. However, at other times, they force themselves to leave because they cannot stop laughing. Their laughter isn't because they aren't concerned with the other individual's wellbeing, it is because something in the action of falling caused them to laugh.

LAUGHTER'S HEALING CAPABILITIES

Nothing releases endorphins from your brain, reduces the level of stress in your body, and strengthens the immune system than laughing. It is proven that laughter therapy, also known as humor therapy, can reduce negativity, emotional stress, and physical discomfort.

1. **Laughter is a natural painkiller**: Laughing produces hormones (happy brain chemicals) that act as a natural painkiller (soothing stress, reducing anxiety, easing chronic pain, and makes a person feel happy).
2. **Strengthens your heart.** Laughing is a cardio activity for the heart because it speeds up a person's heart rate.
3. **Wards off disease**: Laughing is a form of protection for your body. The more you laugh and approach life positively, the fewer chronic diseases you will develop.
4. **Tones your abs**: The action of laughing causes the muscles in your abdomen to contract (or flex) and relax (like when doing Ab crunches).

5. **Boosts immunity**: Laughing activates your body's T-cells (are immune system cells) to help ward off germs and illness.
6. **Decreases blood pressure**: Laughter decreases and maintains healthy blood pressure levels and lowers the risk of a heart attack and stroke.
7. **Banishes stress**: A few moments of laughter will reduce the level of stress hormones (i.e., cortisol) coursing around your abdomen area.
8. **Helps those suffering from depression**: Laughing can improve one's overall outlook on life; and eases emotional and physical discomfort and pain significantly.

COMBAT STRESS

1. **Stimulates many organs:** Laughing enhances your intake of oxygen rich air, stimulates your heart, lungs and muscles, and increases the endorphins released by your brain.
2. **Activate your stress response**: Laughing cools down your stress release and increases your heart rate and decreases your blood pressure, leaving you feeling peaceful and relaxed.
3. **Soothes tension:** Laughing stimulates circulation and aids in muscle relaxation to release some of the physical symptoms of stress.

In every instance where there's laughter, it begins with a SMILE! Smiling activates tiny molecules in your brain that fends off stress and releases dopamine, endorphins and serotonin that lowers your anxiety while increasing feelings of happiness.

Week 25 & 26 Activities

YOUTH ACTIVITIES

Laugh Therapy

LESSON VOCABULARY WORDS

INSTRUCTIONS: Study the vocabulary words listed below for a good understanding of each one.

1. **Shared laughter:** Signals that you see the world the same way as others, boost the sense of connection.
2. **Simulated laughter:** Laughing without experiencing a funny event.

WELLNESS WORKSHEET

1. Make a list of 3 of the funniest movies or TV shows you ever saw to save the world health complications. What would you choose?

   _____
   _____
   _____

2. "Laughter can transport you to a relaxed, positive, and joyful destination. Laughter helps with releasing anger and forgiving sooner." True or False? Why? (Circle your answer.)

   _____
   _____
   _____
   _____

3. Provide examples of individuals whose health and well-being play a huge role in how successful they are. (i.e., Simone Biles, James Harden, Stephen Curry, and JJ Wyatt).

   _____
   _____
   _____
   _____
   _____
   _____
   _____
   _____
   _____

Pillar: Laughing

T-Chart

The past week I laughed at...	I can laugh tomorrow by...

EMPLOYEE OR COMMUNITY CITIZEN ACTIVITIES

Pillar: Laughing

Laugh Therapy

LESSON VOCABULARY WORDS

INSTRUCTIONS: Review vocabulary words listed below with the participants to ensure they have a good understanding of each before starting any of the activities.

1. **CONTAGIOUS LAUGHTER:** a person's laughter causes others to laugh and then you find yourself laughing.

2. **NERVOUS LAUGHTER:** nervous laughter is used to protect a person's dignity and slash or to maintain control of a situation.

3. **CANNED LAUGHTER:** real laughter that is taken completely out of context and place to influence or cause an audience to find humor.

4. **CRUEL LAUGHTER:** is inappropriate, cruel, and insensitive laughter used at another person's expense because something in the action caused them to laugh.

LAUGHING WORKSHEET

Activity 1: From the definitions provided above, select the correct type of laughter for the example: Fill in the blank exercise where the participant determines which scenario goes with the scenario.

(1 Linda is going up the steps and trips. As she is falling, she attempts to brace her fall but breaks her finger. Samantha sees Linda fall and laughs hysterically. Even after hearing she broke her finger, Samantha cannot stop laughing. _____

(2 Tonya walks into the room and everyone stops talking. She walks up to Al and asks what he is eating. Al responds a chicken sandwich and chips and asks Tonya where she is coming from. Tonya laughs before saying she had a meeting wither supervisor. _____

(3 While watching the Kings of Comedy, Marcia begins laughing at Steve Harvey's jokes. Her friend, Tammy, overhears her and begins laughing. Not because she heard the joke but because Marcia was laughing so hard. _____

(4 At the beginning of the Laugh Out Loud Comedy Show, local comedians entertained the audience to get them prepared for the headliners. The audience begin laughing and after a while the whole room was laughing hysterically. _____

(5 _____ can reduce negativity, emotional stress, and physical discomfort.

Activity 2: Fill in the blank with the correct answers from the lesson on the pillar, Learning.

(1 Where there is laughter, it begins with a _____.

(2 _____ is released in the brain when someone laughs.

(3 Pablo Neruda said "laughter is the language of the _____.

(4 Laughing is a _____ activity for the heart because it strengthens the hurt.

(5 _____ and the world _____ with you; _____ and you _____ alone.

Pillar: Laughing

T-Chart

| The past week I laughed at... | I can laugh tomorrow by... |

Week 27 & 28 Activities

YOUTH ACTIVITIES

Anger Management

LESSON VOCABULARY WORDS

INSTRUCTIONS: Study the vocabulary words listed below for a good understanding of each one.

1. **Healthy anger:** Demands reflection and requires that time is taken to exert the effort to empower the rational mind to override the emotional mind.

2. **Anger explosions:** Sudden episodes of impulsive and aggressive behavior.

3. **Emotional triggers:** Statement that may cause you to feel many emotions.

4. **Consequence:** A result or effect of an action or condition.

Pillar: Laughing

WRITING PROMPT TOPIC: Write about 2 experiences that made you angry this week or month, and how you responded to them.

ANGER ICEBERG

INTRODUCTION: Conflicts happen, and when they do, it's important for all parties to have a basic understanding that anger may not be the primary emotion at play. Understanding that anger is often protecting you from the deeper, more vulnerable emotions involved in loss which are more challenging to express can help respond instead of reacting when angered. The iceberg makes you aware that you need to look further into why you are feeling angry and what other emotions have led to the anger you are currently experiencing. And just as important as understanding your own anger is understanding anger that's directed toward you from another. When we recognize another's anger as something deeper, like pain or shame, we can approach conflict more compassionately, without reacting negatively/defensively.

INSTRUCTIONS: Using steps 1 and 2, complete the Anger Iceberg on the next page.

1. **Understand what triggered you.** Ask yourself, where this emotion coming from? (Pay attention to the things, thoughts, feelings and/or experiences that let to your anger.)
2. **Identify what's going on underneath the tip of the iceberg.** Now you can get to the root of the deeper emotion and prioritize that over your anger. You may have to look at past experiences or limiting beliefs you have about yourself. It helps you unpack your anger to understand yourself with more clarity.
3. **Help yourself feel calmer.** Resolve the need to self-soothe and emotionally regulate. Take a walk, focus on some deep breaths, journal, do something physical and/or relax the tension you are experiencing in your body.
4. **Channel your energy.** When our emotions are overwhelming (and confusing) us, it can be difficult to focus on anything else. Understanding them will help you channel that energy into things you'd rather focus on, volunteer at a charity/charitable organization, go running/jogging, workout, ride a bike, etc.

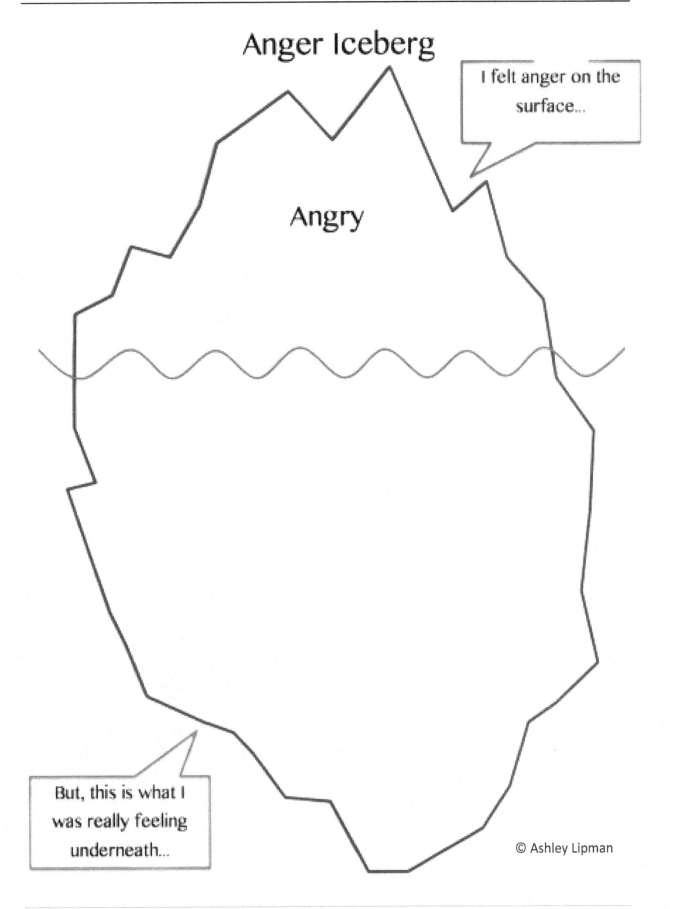

5 Yoga Poses to Release Anger:

1. **Easy Seated Pose (Sukhasana) With Breath of Fire**

   Find Sukhasana, or Easy Seated Pose, and take a moment to feel grounded and connected to the earth here. This simple step of mindfulness will help center you and start pulling you from the grips of anger.

   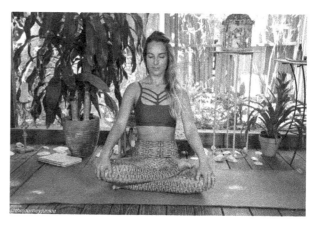

   Now you're ready to practice **Breath of Fire Pranayama** for a full 60 seconds. Commit to releasing any built-up anger that you have been suppressing. Allow that anger to rise to the surface and as you exhale, let it go. *Not Sure How to Practice? Here's a Breath of Fire Pranayama Tutorial.* When you're done, open your palms and stretch your arms overhead. This provides a direct channel to release your anger. If you feel like you have any lingering emotions, scream for a few seconds to let it go.

   Screaming therapy, also known as **primal therapy**, is scientifically proven to be good for your health. So go ahead and let it all out! You'll feel better after you do. Then, let your arms fall down by your sides and sit in silence for a few minutes. Notice how you feel. Is there a shift in your emotional state? Do you feel like a weight has been lifted?

   How it helps release anger: Sukhasana helps you get grounded, which is the first step in releasing negative emotions. Breath of Fire deeply focuses the mind, detoxifies the body, and shifts the energy so you can let. it. go.

2. **Camel Pose (Ustrasana)**

   Begin in a kneeling position with your hips stacked over your knees. Place your palms against your low back, bringing your elbows in toward the center of your back. Begin to gently press your hips forward as you lift from the chest and send your gaze towards the ceiling.

   You can stay here. If Camel Pose is part of your practice and you'd like to take the final expression, slowly reach down, and grab your heels with each hand.

   Not Sure How to Practice? Here's How to Access Camel Pose Safely

   Wherever you are, stay there for five deep breaths. When you're ready, come out of Camel Pose slowly and rest your seat to your heels. Bring your hands into your lap and sit quietly with your eyes

Pillar: Laughing

open (so you don't get dizzy) breathing deeply for another 5-10 breaths, noticing how you feel both emotionally and physically.

How it helps release anger:

Camel Pose is a big heart opener. Heart openers activate the Heart Chakra, inviting in and sending out love, helping to melt away the anger.

3. **Revolved Crescent Lunge (Parivrtta Anjaneyasana)**

Start in Low Crescent Lunge Pose with your right foot forward. Bring your hands to heart center and keeping your spine lengthened, hinge your torso forward slightly as you hook your left elbow to the outside of your right knee.

Option to push your elbow against the outside of your leg for a deeper twist. Make sure your shoulders are relaxed away from your ears. Slowly straighten into your back leg (you can keep a micro bend in your back knee) and press down through your back left heel. As you twist, pull in your lower abdomen, and lift your torso away from your thigh. Stay in this pose for 30-60 seconds (or longer if it's part of your practice), and then repeat on the other side.

How it helps release anger:

Twists nourish and massage the spinal column. When we're angry, we physically become closed off, rounding the spine and creating tension in the body. This twist helps release tension so you can then release your anger.

4. **Goddess Pose (Utkata Konasana) with Ganesha Mudra**

Mudras, which translates to "seal" in Sanskrit, are symbolic gestures of the hands to support the flow of energy within the body. Different parts of the hands are linked to different areas in the body and brain.

Common Mudras, Their Meaning, and How to Practice Them

By placing our hands in mudras, we stimulate specific areas, which can alter our state of mind. The Ganesha Mudra, named after the Hindu elephant deity who removes obstacles, is believed to help alleviate anger. Start in Goddess Pose with your heels in, toes out, and knees gently pressing outward. Bring your left hand in front of your sternum, palm facing outward with your thumb pointing down. Bring your right hand in front of the left, palm facing toward you, with your thumb pointing up. Bend your fingers and hook the right fingers with the left fingers, your elbows pointing outward. Inhale deeply and as you exhale, pull your elbows away from one another, keeping your fingers interlocked. Take five deep breaths here.

How it helps release anger:

The Ganesha Mudra combined with Goddess Pose promotes better blood circulation and releases tension in the shoulders and chest, helping to open up the Heart Chakra.

Goddess Pose also opens the hips and cultivates confidence and strength so you can release your anger and move on.

5. **Corpse Pose (Savasana)**

   As a pose of total relaxation and deep restoration, Savasana is a great way to complete your yoga to release anger practice.

   To begin, lie on your back with your legs extended long and arms by your sides with your palms facing up. Keep your eyes closed, breathe naturally and allow your body to sink into the mat – from the tips of your toes all the way up to your eyebrows and forehead, fully relax and soften. Starting from the soles of your feet and moving to the top of your head, release any lingering tension. Invite peace and calm into your mind, body and spirit. Stay in this position for five minutes.

   How it helps release anger:

   Practicing Savasana helps you rejuvenate and recharge by activating the parasympathetic nervous system, also known as the "rest and digest" reaction in the body. This pose lowers blood pressure and heart rate, which is particularly beneficial when it comes to releasing anger.

EMPLOYEE OR COMMUNITY CITIZEN ACTIVITIES

Anger Management

LESSON VOCABULARY WORDS

INSTRUCTIONS: Study the vocabulary words listed below for a good understanding of each one.

1. **Healthy anger:** Demands reflection and requires that time is taken to exert the effort to empower the rational mind to override the emotional mind.

2. **Anger explosions:** Sudden episodes of impulsive and aggressive behavior.

3. **Emotional triggers:** Statement that may cause you to feel many emotions.

4. **Consequence:** A result or effect of an action or condition.

Pillar: Laughing

WRITING PROMPT TOPIC: Write about 2 experiences that made you angry this week or month, and how you responded to them.

ANGER ICEBERG

INTRODUCTION: conflicts happen, and when they do, it's important for all parties to have a basic understanding that anger may not be the primary emotion at play. Understanding that anger is often protecting you from the deeper, more vulnerable emotions involved in loss which are more challenging to express can help respond instead of reacting when angered. The iceberg makes you aware that you need to look further into why you are feeling angry and what other emotions have led to the anger you are currently experiencing. And just as important as understanding your own anger is understanding anger that's directed toward you from another. When we recognize another's anger as something deeper, like pain or shame, we can approach conflict more compassionately, without reacting negatively/defensively.

Instructions: Using steps 1 and 2, complete the Anger Iceberg on the next page.

1. **Understand what triggered you.** Ask yourself, where this emotion coming from? (Pay attention to the things, thoughts, feelings and/or experiences that let to your anger.)

2. **Identify what's going on underneath the tip of the iceberg.** Now you can get to the root of the deeper emotion and prioritize that over your anger. You may have to look at past experiences or limiting beliefs you have about yourself. It helps you unpack your anger to understand yourself with more clarity.

3. **Help yourself feel calmer.** Resolve the need to self-soothe and emotionally regulate. Take a walk, focus on some deep breaths, journal, do something physical and/or relax the tension you are experiencing in your body.

4. **Channel your energy.** When our emotions are overwhelming (and confusing) us, it can be difficult to focus on anything else. Understanding them will help you channel that energy into things you'd rather focus on, volunteer at a charity/charitable organization, go running/jogging, workout, ride a bike, etc.

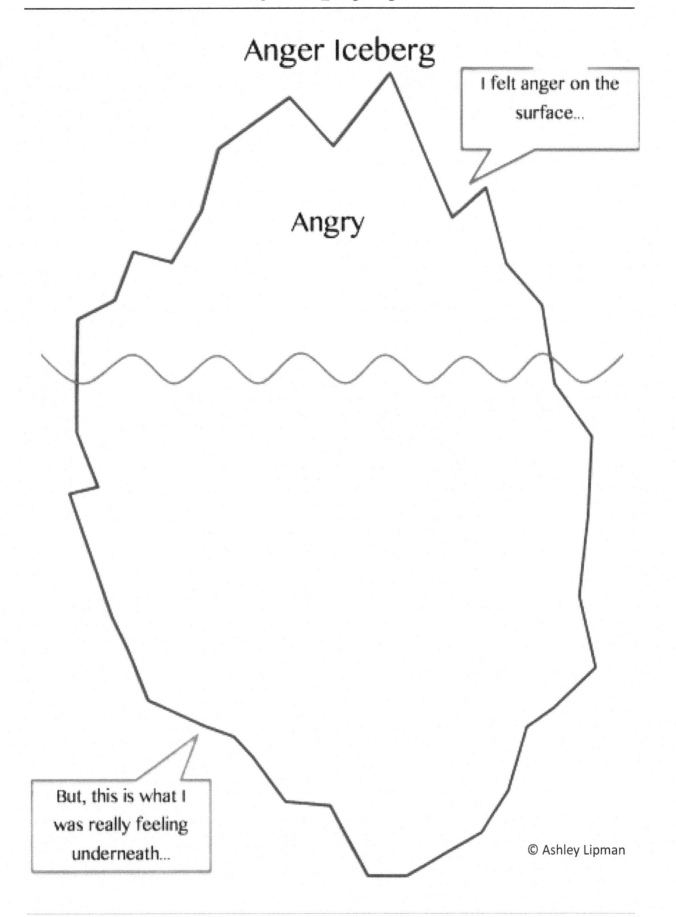

Week 29 & 30 Activities

YOUTH ACTIVITIES

Overcoming Stress and Anxiety

LESSON VOCABULARY WORDS

INSTRUCTIONS: Review vocabulary words listed below with the participants to ensure they have a good understanding of each before starting any of the activities.

1. **Stress:** A state of mental or emotional strain or tension resulting from adverse or very demanding circumstances.

2. **Anxiety:** A feeling of worry, nervousness, or unease, typically about an imminent event or something with an uncertain outcome.

3. **False front:** Putting forth a vision of yourself to someone that is anything other than the pure, undistorted truth.

WHAT DO OTHERS THINK OF ME VS WHAT I KNOW ABOUT ME CHART

Activity 1: Complete the chart below using the 3 examples provided:

a. When I get in trouble at home or school.
b. When I stay out past my curfew or the time I was told to be home by.
c. When I am disrespectful and will not listen.

Activity 2: Answer the following by responding true or false to each statement:

1. _____ Only adults get stressed and deal with anxiety.

2. _____ Stress and anxiety are the same.

3. _____ Stress and anxiety aren't real.

What do other people think of me?	What do I know of me?	Who am I working to become?

Pillar: Laughing

Mindful Morning

5 — Slowly take five deep breaths.
☐ ☐ ☐ ☐ ☐

4 — List four things you can see or notice around you.

3 — List three things you are grateful for.

2 — Say two positive self-talk statements to yourself.

1 — Name one thing you are looking forward to today.

© 2020 Pathway 2 Success

JOURNAL PAGES

Pillar: Laughing

EMPLOYEE OR COMMUNITY CITIZEN ACTIVITIES

Overcoming Stress and Anxiety

LESSON VOCABULARY WORDS

INSTRUCTIONS: Review vocabulary words listed below with the participants to ensure they have a good understanding of each before starting any of the activities.

1. **Stress:** A state of mental or emotional strain or tension resulting from adverse or very demanding circumstances.

2. **Anxiety:** A feeling of worry, nervousness, or unease, typically about an imminent event or something with an uncertain outcome.

3. **False front:** Putting forth a vision of yourself to someone that is anything other than the pure, undistorted truth.

Pillar: Laughing

OVERCOMING STRESS AND ANXIETY

4 Better Ways to Respond to "How Are You?"

1. **My day has been great so far.** [Give a reason why]. When you're genuinely enthusiastic, it's truly difficult for others to resist your good mood. And note that your reason doesn't have to be incredibly impressive. You might say, "Thanks for asking! I'm having a great day."

2. **I'll be honest—I've had better days. Hopefully, tomorrow will be better!** Unless you're speaking to a total stranger, don't be afraid to be honest. Having a terrible day is hard enough—trying to cover it up can be even worse. Oftentimes, being a little vulnerable with people strengthens the relationship (and you never know when they'll say, "Ugh, me too! What's going on with the universe today?!?") As long as you end on a slightly optimistic note—like, "tomorrow will be better"—sharing the less-good times is definitely kosher.

3. **Good, thank you. I'm just** [appreciating/looking forward to]… This response lets you acknowledge something you're happy about. The other person will appreciate your cheery response. Even better, it gives them something to ask you about.

4. **Hmmm…productive. Thanks for asking**! How are you? Sometimes, you're running around like crazy trying to get everything done. That probably means you're stressed—so you might not feel like saying you feel great. This response also gives the other person a chance to ask, "What have you been doing?" Discussing your current projects with your coworkers or friends is a great way to learn more about each other's work lives and even get suggestions or ideas.

(https://www.sigconsult.com/blog/2019/02/4-better-ways-to-respond-to-how-are-you-than-im-good?source=google.com)

Activity 1: What is workplace anxiety?

(1 What causes workplace anxiety? (Select the best answer.)
- a. Deadlines
- b. Interpersonal relationships/Workplace Bullying
- c. Staff management
- d. Arisen issues/problems
- e. No being able to take a smoke break
- f. All of the above.
- g. None of the above.

(2 _____ can interfere with productivity and impact physical and emotional health.

(3 What/Who is the one thing that's always within your control?

_____

_____

Activity 2: Make a list of ways you can combat workplace anxiety/stress.

Pillar: Laughing

PTSD: TOP 5 SIGNS OF PTSD YOU NEED TO KNOW

Posted on 03/05/18 01:36:pm

According to the National Center for PTSD, posttraumatic stress disorder, about 8 million Americans have PTSD during any given year. While the signs of PTSD in women don't differ greatly from signs of PTSD in men, women are more likely to develop PTSD, with a lifetime incidence of 1 in 10. For men, it's 1 in 25. Yet an even higher number of Americans experience and show signs of trauma each year. So when does suffering a traumatic event lead to suffering from PTSD?

"PTSD is a mental health diagnosis characterized by five events or symptoms," says Dr. Chad Wetterneck, PhD, clinical supervisor for Rogers Behavioral Health. Here, Dr. Wetterneck walks us through each sign of PTSD:

1. **A life-threatening event.** This includes a perceived-to-be life threatening event. Whether or not it actually is, it's really about the perception of the person who experienced or witnessed the event that it could happen to them again.

2. **Internal reminders of a traumatic event.** These signs of trauma typically present as nightmares or flashbacks. It's important to realize that these are not simply memories. They are unwanted, intrusive episodes in which a person feels as though they are in the life-threatening situation again – like they're watching a movie or seeing it unfold in front of them. It feels very real to them.

3. **Avoidance of external reminders.** Those with PTSD often do whatever they can to not think about their traumatic event, to suppress the feelings associated with it. They might avoid alleys if they were assaulted in one, or they might refuse to drive if they were in a car accident.

4. **Altered anxiety state.** PTSD can leave people feeling on edge and looking out for danger (hypervigilance). Really, what it boils down to is that people feel more anxious. Their startle response is exaggerated. They're jumpy or looking over their shoulder more often. It's a physical sign of PTSD and reaction to the body's increased anxiety and the need to be aware of possible threats.

5. **Changes in mood or thinking.** People with PTSD can see the world as a very dangerous place. And because they focus on protecting themselves from it, it's often difficult for them to go out in public. The isolation can lead to depression, or sometimes a person may act in an opposite way when they see no future. In that case, they may take more risks or engage in risky behaviors.

"While we are continuing to learn more about it's complicated symptoms and diagnosis, there is no 'cure' for PTSD— we cannot fully remove a traumatic memory from the brain," says Dr. Wetterneck. *"However, there are proven treatments that greatly reduce the symptoms and help people move forward with healthy lives."*

Concerned you or a loved one may be suffering from the signs of trauma or PTSD? You can take a short, confidential quiz to check your symptoms. If you believe you or a loved one needs help, please request a free screening online or give us a call at 800-767-4411.

(https://rogersbh.org/about-us/newsroom/blog/ptsd-5-signs-you-need-know)

Mindfulness Time!

Issue Number 1

NAME: _____

Joke of the Day: Where does a waitress with only one leg work?
Answer: IHOP
Grade: _____

Grade the joke above: A+ or D- ?

Thought for Today

"Remember that stress does not come from what is going on in your life. It comes from your thoughts about what is going on in your life."
-Andrew Bernstein

My rating for this quote = ____ /10

List your top 3 goals for today in the space below.

1.

2.

3.

Draw a picture of a face that is representative of how you are feeling today.

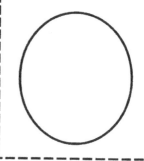

The Big Question!

When I am feeling stressed out, who can I turn to for support and comfort?

Make a sentence where each word begins with these letters in order:

O_____ K_____ T_____ R_____ F_____

List 5 positive attributes or personal characteristics that you have.

1.

2.

3.

4.

5.

Draw a picture that combines these two words: Shrek and Acceptance.

JOURNAL PAGES

Pillar: Laughing

Week 31 & 32 Activities

YOUTH ACTIVITIES

Express Yourself

LESSON VOCABULARY WORDS

INSTRUCTIONS: Review vocabulary words listed below with the participants to ensure they have a good understanding of each before starting any of the activities.

1. **Self-Awareness:** Conscious knowledge of one's own character, feelings, motives, and desires.

2. **Self-Expression:** The expression of one's feelings, thoughts, or ideas, especially in writing, art, music, or dance.

3. **Self-Representation:** The way we represent ourselves to others within a particular culture.

Pillar: Laughing

"WHAT WOULD YOU DO?" ACTIVITY

INSTRUCTIONS: After watching the video clip, answer the following questions:

1. What is the video about?

   _____

   _____

   _____

2. Why is there an issue? And what is the issue?

   _____

   _____

   _____

3. How is the topic impacting the characters' lives?

   _____

   _____

   _____

4. What does each participant have to say about the subject of the video?

   _____

   _____

   _____

JOURNAL PAGES

Pillar: Laughing

EMPLOYEE OR COMMUNITY CITIZEN ACTIVITIES

Express Yourself

LESSON VOCABULARY WORDS

INSTRUCTIONS: Study the vocabulary words listed below for a good understanding of each one.

1. **Self-Awareness:** Conscious knowledge of one's own character, feelings, motives, and desires.

2. **Self-Expression:** The expression of one's feelings, thoughts, or ideas, especially in writing, art, music, or dance.

3. **Self-Representation:** The way we represent ourselves to others within a particular culture.

WHAT IS WORKPLACE BULLYING?

Workplace bullying is harmful, targeted behavior that happens at work. It might be spiteful, offensive, mocking, or intimidating. It forms a pattern, and it tends to be directed at one person or a few people.

A few examples of bullying include:

- targeted practical jokes
- being purposely misled about work duties, like incorrect deadlines or unclear directions
- continued denial of requests for time off without an appropriate or valid reason
- threats, humiliation, and other verbal abuse
- excessive performance monitoring
- overly harsh or unjust criticism

Criticism or monitoring isn't always bullying. For example, objective and constructive criticism and disciplinary action directly related to workplace behavior or job performance aren't considered bullying.

But criticism meant to intimidate, humiliate, or single someone out without reason would be considered bullying. According to the Workplace Bullying Institute, more than 60 million working people in the United States are affected by bullying. Existing federal and state laws only protect workers against bullying when it involves physical harm or when the target belongs to a protected group, such as people living with disabilities or people of color. Since bullying is often verbal or psychological in nature, it may not always be visible to others. Read on to learn more about ways to identify workplace bullies, how workplace bullying can affect you, and safe actions you can take against bullying. Identifying workplace bullying

Bullying can be subtle. One helpful way to identify bullying is to consider how others might view what's happening. This can depend, at least partially, on the circumstances. But if most people would see a specific behavior as unreasonable, it's generally bullying.

TYPES OF BULLYING

Bullying behaviors might be:

- **Verbal.** This could include mockery, humiliation, jokes, gossip, or other spoken abuse.
- **Intimidating.** This might include threats, social exclusion in the workplace, spying, or other invasions of privacy.
- **Related to work performance.** Examples include wrongful blame, work sabotage or interference, or stealing or taking credit for ideas.
- **Retaliatory.** In some cases, talking about the bullying can lead to accusations of lying, further exclusion, refused promotions, or other retaliation.
- **Institutional.** Institutional bullying happens when a workplace accepts, allows, and even encourages bullying to take place. This bullying might include unrealistic production goals, forced overtime, or singling out those who can't keep up.

Bullying behavior is repeated over time. This sets it apart from harassment, which is often limited to a single instance. Persistent harassment can become bullying, but since harassment refers to actions toward a protected group of people, it's illegal, unlike bullying.

Early warning signs of bullying can vary:

- Co-workers might become quiet or leave the room when you walk in, or they might simply ignore you.
- You might be left out of office culture, such as chitchat, parties, or team lunches.
- Your supervisor or manager might check on you often or ask you to meet multiple times a week without a clear reason.
- You may be asked to do new tasks or tasks outside your typical duties without training or help, even when you request it.
- It may seem like your work is frequently monitored, to the point where you begin to doubt yourself and have difficulty with your regular tasks.
- You might be asked to do difficult or seemingly pointless tasks and be ridiculed or criticized when you can't get them done.
- You may notice a pattern of your documents, files, other work-related items, or personal belongings going missing.

These incidents may seem random at first. If they continue, you may worry something you did caused them and fear you'll be fired or demoted. Thinking about work, even on your time off, may cause anxiety and dread. (https://www.healthline.com/health/workplace-bullying#What-is-workplace-bullying?)

WRITE A LETTER TO YOUR 12-YEAR-OLD SELF

INSTRUCTIONS: Make a list of 4-5 things you would like to say to your 12-year-old self and create a letter that will help build his/her self-esteem, self-image, and overall concept of self. Knowing what you know now, what would you say to him/her?

Pillar: Laughing

Pillar: Laughing

PILLAR: LEADING

PILLAR: LEADING

Before anyone can become a leader of many, they must first become a leader of one: SELF. The core values the mentee has learned while on this journey are invaluable and transferable. However, to become an effective leader, the mentee must develop or enhance their leadership skills. Leadership is about serving others and isn't self-serving. As we step into these lessons on LEADERSHIP, I challenge you not to lose sight of the self-work you have already done. That work should begin revealing the mentee's life plan and the journey he/she is to take. Some people are natural born leaders while others are taught to be leaders. Regardless which category the mentee falls into, to be an effective leader he/she must be concerned with people and their ability to learn the core values, systems, and processes that are the nuts and bolts of the company or organization in which they work. The expectations, skills and tools needed to secure a successful education; and their personal values, insight, and willingness to serve others are all the framework of an effective leader.

This pillar on leading begins first with the mentor before the mentee enters the picture. The mentor MUST understand that to be an effective leader, he/she must serve. John Maxwell shares his leadership philosophy as "*One life influencing another. This is the heart of leadership. One person casting vision. One person forging legacy, so that their influence incites the same passion in those they seek to lead. Afterall, people are our most valuable asset.* [Affording] ...*you the power to impact those lives, to motivate teams, to transform organizations... We believe leadership is a process marked by constant growth.*" (*John Maxwell on Leadership*, https://www.td.org/magazines/td-magazine/john-maxwell-on-leadership, by ATD Staff, February 8, 2013). Mentoring is the truest form of leadership any person can participate in. Leadership, in a nutshell, takes everything covered in the previous pillars and brings it into perspective for the mentor to understand their role in the mentor-mentee relationship. In the article, *Develop Leadership Skills with a Mentor*, (https://www.togetherplatform.com/blog/mentoring-develop-leadership-skills-with-a-mentor, by Matthew Reeves, August 1, 2021) the author says, "*Mentorship. Leaders learn through direct experience and the advice of others… mentors provide role models and guidance that future leaders can aspire to be like. Mentorship, in short, builds leadership skills.*" The mentor's ability to see past their hopes, dreams, and desires to serve as a life or career guide to another person identifies within themselves their leadership qualities. The same qualities that will be modeled in front of the mentee as they learn how to navigate their journey called life. Tony Dungy shared in the *4 Essential Traits* of a Mentor Leader, (https://www.allprodad.com/4-essential-traits-of-a-mentor-leader/) *"In my life and career, I have seen all kinds of leaders. The ones who have had the greatest positive impact on my life are the select few who have been not only leaders, but also mentors. Here are four essential traits of a mentor leader to keep in mind:*

1. *Becoming a mentor leader is not rocket science. Leadership comprises of principles and skills that are accessible to anyone and everyone. They aren't necessarily intuitive, but they aren't terribly difficult, either.*
2. *Mentor leadership can be taught and learned; but in order to be absorbed, it must be practiced. The best way to evaluate leadership philosophies and find your own style is by testing them in action.*
3. *Mentor leadership focuses on developing the strengths of individuals. It might be in a narrowing way, such as building a specific skill, or more broadly focused, such as teaching employees to be proactive about meeting others' needs so they can better support the organization. Successful mentor leaders make the people they lead better players, workers, students, or family members and, ultimately, better people.*
4. *Mentor leadership works best when the ones being mentored are aware that the mentor leader has a genuine concern for their development and success. Those we lead will be more receptive if they believe we genuinely want them to succeed."*

As I was reading through Tony's essential mentor leadership traits, I thought about the many mentors I have had throughout my life and career, and how each of them instilled something in me I still use today. The same journey I took to get to where I am today, is the same journey mentors will take mentees to help them maximize the mentoring experience and take the skills they've gained, lessons they have learned and the experience that have totally changed their lives to become the best version of themselves possible. As Tony said, "*...this isn't rocket science...,*" it is an opportunity to give back and to impart knowledge into another person who helps them see beyond their limitations into the expansive world which is theirs to experience however they deem necessary.

ROLE MODELING

The article, *Positive role models and mentors have an important role to play in promoting pro-environmental behaviors*, (https://research.childrenandnature.org/research/positive-role-models-and-mentors-have-an-important-role-to-play-in-promoting-pro-environmental-behaviors/, Prince, H.E.,

(2017). Outdoor experiences and sustainability. Journal of Adventure Education and Outdoor Learning, 17(2), 161-171.) says, *"Social learning theory includes the idea that people learn behaviors by observing others. This theory supports the utilization of role models and mentors in educational programs designed to influence the behaviors of children and youth."* The article goes on to say, *"Through role modeling, mentoring, and coaching, educators can also promote students' sense of empowerment and commitment to sustainability. Effective mentorship provides benefits for both the mentor and mentee. The mentee gains increased confidence and skill, while the mentor experiences renewed enthusiasm."*

To better understand the role of the mentor and an important aspect of their mentor-mentee relationship, let's inspect what a role model is. According to *Role Model vs. Mentor: Compare & Contrast,* https://study.com/academy/lesson/role-model-vs-mentor-compare-contrast.html, by Artem Cheprasov) *"A role model is an individual whose example, such as their behaviors or successes, are looked up to and imitated by others… Mentors are like personal role models. More formally, we can state that mentors are trusted individuals with more experience and wisdom than another person who helps guide that person with respect to a particular concern or desire. There is a personal, two-way relationship here. Mentors want to see you succeed, while role models may not even know who you are!* As I was reading this article, it became apparent that a mentor MUST choose to be a role-model and model the behavior, attributes and/or abilities of a leader in front of their mentee for them to observe it, internalize it and model it in their daily life. In the chapter on LEARNING, *I shared, "LEARNING only happens where we see the value in acquiring or obtaining the information for internal or external use. Sometimes the information is only valuable to you because of your own personal values and the accomplishments you desire for your life. [It provides] the freedom to make a decision that changed their perspective regarding the situation and make the decision that was the right one for them in that moment."* Think about that for a moment! In the same way that a mentee determines which information offered by the mentor is valuable, the mentor must determine what information to share that will be of value to the mentee. That alone can change the mentee's perspective, behaviors and/or attitude toward life, school, their community, and the world. That's the power of mentors being a role model and leading their mentees by example. They take the best they have to offer and that is relevant in that moment. The mentor has the potential of impacting their mentee's life in a way that empowers and enables them to activate and model what they have observed and learned.

LEADERSHIP SKILLS/QUALITIES

Now that we have spoken to the mentor, let's talk about the information that will help the mentor equip and empower the mentee to step into the role of a leader as a result of participating in an effective and successful mentoring program. As we discuss leadership qualities, the mentor is to impart to the mentee keep in mind that "...*mentoring is a process for the informal transmission of knowledge, social capital and the psychosocial support perceived by the recipient as relevant to work, career or professional development; mentoring entails informal communication, usually face-to-face and during a sustained period of time, between a person who is perceived to have greater relevant knowledge, wisdom or experience (the mentor) and a person who is perceived to have less (the protégé or mentee)*." (*Develop Leadership Skills by Mentoring*, https://www.reliableplant.com/Read/29332/mentoring-develops-leadership, by Debbie Zmorenski, from excerpt by Bozeman, Feeney, 2007,)

1. **COMMUNICATION.** Having excellent communication skills is an essential leadership competency. The best leaders are skilled communicators who can communicate in a variety of ways, from transmitting information to inspire others to coaching direct reports. And you must be able to listen to, and communicate with, a wide range of people across roles, geographies, social identities, and more.

2. **TIME-MANAGEMENT.** Time has a monetary value today. Time-management requires a person to organize and prioritize tasks to be more effective with consideration to any competing priorities.

3. **CRITICAL THINKING.** Critical thinking is one of the topmost important skills required of successful leaders. Critical thinkers are intelligent decision makers, highly analytical and always rational. A leader must be able to stand firm on his/her decisions. Because he/she is a critical thinker, it should be safe to assume that every decision he/she makes is well researched, objectively scrutinized and that all potential outcomes were assessed, and therefore, their eventual choice is the best course of action.

4. **RESPECT.** In today's society, there seems to be a misnomer that states ***to get respect, you must give respect***. Although that may be the way of the world. It is not the sign of a good leader. A good leader gives respect understanding that by doing so, he/she is teaching others how to respect and treat them. Respect is inherent (*existing in something as a permanent, essential*).

It is not about the absence of disrespect, but about how a leader can INFLUENCE (*authentically and transparently being able to convince people through logical, emotional, or cooperative appeals*) others while building and sustaining mutually beneficial relationships that are built on a foundation of RESPECT.)

5. **LEARNING AGILITY.** A leader who has learned the importance of being a life learner is one who learns from their mistakes and those of others, seek opportunities to grow while asking insightful and informative questions, and are open to hear other's opinions and feedback on relevant topics. This leader realizes that there are truly no failures in life, only opportunities to learn how to do something more efficiently and/or differently. This includes recognizing when new behaviors, leadership skills, and/or attitudes are needed and seeking opportunities to develop them.

6. **CHANGE MANAGEMENT AND INNOVATION SKILLS.** Change happens whether or not you want it to and being able to manage change in both your life and in business is essential when leading yourself and people. Wikipedia defines change management as a *collective term for all approaches to prepare, support and help individuals, teams, and organizations in making organizational or structural change.* Before change can occur, there must be some sign that change is needed. I think Oprah said it best, *"The greatest discovery of all time is that a person can change his future by merely changing his attitude."* Think about that for a moment. Change happens every second of every day, whether or not we acknowledge it. It singularly can usher an individual into the next season of life or be the reason they are left behind because they refuse to accept and do what is necessary to manifest it in their life. This is an aspect of being a life learner (Learning Agility) especially when a leader recognizes *"...when new behaviors, leadership skills, and/or attitudes are needed and [seeks] opportunities to develop them."* That's when genuine change happens!

7. **SERVICE-MINDED.** A servant leader feels responsible to help people learn and grow, feel purposeful, motivated, and energized, as he/she contributes to the betterment of the people and not merely selfish gain. He/She realizes this calling isn't about him/her but about the people! Simply put, servant leaders have the humility, insight, and courage to accept, acknowledge and understand that their greatest lessons have come from the people they interact with and/or surround themselves with. Leaders understand that as they accept their right to their views and/or opinions they must also do so with others simply because they are

a member of humanity. A servant leader searches for opportunities to serve others with the understanding that before he/she can effectively serve anyone else, they MUST first be a servant to themselves. Malcolm X said, "*We can't teach what we don't know, and we can't LEAD where we can't* [or won't] *go.*" The following are some significant attributes of a service-minded leader (*6 Reasons Why Servant Leadership is Best*, https://www.rootinc.com/why-servant-leadership-really-works/, by Jim Haudan, October 26, 2020):

a. **Encourages others to think for themselves**. It is not that we don't know. Sometimes we must talk it out to hear the solution as we speak. Which builds character, and confidence in themselves and their abilities while helping them realize their place in the world.

b. **Believe that all people are valuable and have something great to contribute**. He/She refuses to believe that anyone has the right or should throw people away as irrelevant. A service-minded leader builds trust with others from the care and genuine concern they show regularly. He/She believes in investing in people in the same way that others have invested in him/her.

c. **Lives their life of service by asking one question: How may I help?** This question empowers people to step up and say what they need help with. It "*...highlights the best in others, which will create far better results than if the leader dictated directions from their removed perspective. Servant leaders believe this approach reveals the untapped creative and performance capabilities of* [all] *people...*" (*Servant Leader as Change Agents - A Lean Journey*, by Tim McMahon, April 11, 2022, http://www.aleanjourney.com/2022/04/servant-leader-as-change-agents.html) This is necessary, regardless if the mentee is a youth, frontline employee, and/or community worker.

Week 33 & 34 Activities

YOUTH ACTIVITIES

Pillar: Leading

Leading Social Change

LESSON VOCABULARY WORDS

INSTRUCTIONS: Study the vocabulary words listed below for a good understanding of each one.

1. **Social movement-** an organized effort by a large number of people to bring about or impede social, political, economic, or cultural change. There are five types of social movements.

2. **Reform movement-** movement that seeks some sort of change to some aspect of a nation's political, economic, or social systems. The goal is to improve conditions within the nation's current regime, not overthrow.

3. **Self-help movements-** movement that involves people trying to improve aspects of their personal lives; examples of self-help groups include Alcoholics Anonymous and Weight Watchers.

4. **Religious movements-** a movement started to reinforce religious beliefs among their members and to convert other people to these beliefs.

5. **Reactionary movement-** a movement initiated to block social change or to reverse social changes that have already been achieved.

6. **Revolutionary movement-** a movement that want to replace already existing orders with a totally different structure.

SOCIAL MOVEMENTS

1. **Women's Movement**: The feminist movement (also known as the women's movement, or feminism) refers to a series of social movements and Political campaigns for radical and liberal reforms on women's issues created by the inequality between men and women.
2. **Disability Rights Movement**: a global movement that advocates for and secures equal rights and opportunities for people who have disabilities. In the United States, and around the world, the movement has been successful in changing laws and social attitudes to make societies more inclusive.
3. **LGBT Movement**: Lesbian, gay, bisexual, and transgender (LGBT) movements are social movements that advocate for LGBT people in society. Some focus on equal rights, such as the ongoing movement for same-sex marriage, while others focus on liberation, as in the gay liberation movement of the 1960s and 1970s.
4. **Environmental Movement**: (sometimes referred to as the ecology movement) is a diverse philosophical, social, and political movement for addressing environmental issues.
5. **Labor Movement**: consists of two main wings: the trade union movement (British English) or labor union movement (American English) on the one hand, and the political labor movement on the other. Consists of the collective organization of working people developed to represent and campaign for better working conditions and treatment from their employers and, by the implementation of labor and employment laws, from their governments. The standard unit of organization is the trade union. A political party that represents the interests of employees.
6. **Reproductive Justice Movement**: is the human right to maintain personal bodily autonomy, have children, not have children, and parent the children we have in safe and sustainable communities. The reproductive justice framework encompasses a wide range of issues affecting the reproductive lives of marginalized women, including access to: contraception, comprehensive sex education, prevention and care for sexually transmitted infections, alternative birth options, adequate prenatal and pregnancy care, domestic violence assistance, adequate wages to support families, and safe homes.
7. **Anti-War Movement**: is a social movement, usually in opposition to a particular nation's decision to start or carry on an armed conflict, unconditional of a maybe-existing just cause. It is also the opposition to all use of military force during conflicts, or to anti-war books, paintings, and other works of art.

SOCIAL MOVEMENT QUESTIONS

1. What are some issues in your community that you would like to address, change and/or improve?

   _____

   _____

2. How would you go about addressing those issues? How can you have a positive impact on your community?

   _____

   _____

Pillar: Leading

SOCIAL MOVEMENTS WORKSHEET

Junior Scholastic
SKILLS SHEET   Name: Date:

Analyzing a Primary Source

Why We Can't Wait

KEY STANDARD RH.6-8.1

Before he was assassinated on April 4, 1968, civil rights leader Martin Luther King Jr. was jailed dozens of times in his pursuit of racial equality in the United States.

One of those jailings occurred in April 1963 in Birmingham, Alabama. King described Birmingham in the 1960s as "the most thoroughly segregated city in the United States." Rather than integrate its public parks and playgrounds, the city closed them. And opponents of civil rights for African Americans bombed black homes and businesses.

In the spring of 1963, King and other civil rights leaders converged on Birmingham to organize demonstrations against the inequality and violence. King's actions landed him in Birmingham City Jail, where he wrote one of the most important documents of the civil rights movement. The 21-page, 7,000-word *Letter From Birmingham Jail* was written in response to a group of white religious leaders who asked African Americans to wait patiently for equal rights.

Read this excerpt from King's letter, then answer the questions.

Letter From Birmingham Jail, April 16, 1963

My Dear Fellow Clergymen:

While confined here in the Birmingham City Jail, I came across your recent statement calling my present activities "unwise and untimely." . . .

We know through painful experience that freedom is never voluntarily given by the oppressor; it must be demanded by the oppressed. . . . For years now I have heard the word "Wait!" It rings in the ear of every Negro* with piercing familiarity. This "Wait" has almost always meant "Never." We must come to see . . . that "justice too long delayed is justice denied."

We have waited for more than 340 years for our constitutional and God-given rights. The nations of Asia and Africa are moving with jetlike speed toward gaining political independence, but we still creep at horse-and-buggy pace toward gaining a cup of coffee at a lunch counter.

Perhaps it is easy for those who have never felt the stinging darts of segregation to say, "Wait." But when you have seen vicious mobs lynch your mothers and fathers at will and drown your sisters and brothers at whim; when you have seen hate-filled policemen curse, kick, and even kill your black brothers and sisters; when you see the vast majority of your 20 million Negro brothers smothering in an airtight cage of poverty . . . then you will understand why we find it difficult to wait.

There comes a time when the cup of endurance runs over, and men are no longer willing to be plunged into the abyss of despair. I hope, sirs, you can understand our legitimate and unavoidable impatience. . . .

Yours for the cause of Peace and Brotherhood,
Martin Luther King Jr.

*African American (Once a standard term, *Negro* is now considered dated and often offensive.)

Questions

1. What does Martin Luther King Jr. think *wait* means for African Americans? Cite evidence from the text.
2. What metaphors does King use to describe segregation and living in poverty?
3. Compare and contrast King's observations of progress in Asia and Africa with that in the United States. What comment is he making about the U.S.?
4. What examples of racial violence does King include in his letter?
5. What descriptive language does King use to show that African Americans were tired of waiting for racial equality?

https://junior.scholastic.com/pages/content-hubs/the-civil-rights-movement.html

Intentional Mentoring Mentee's Workbook

Name _____ Date _____

Crossword Puzzle:
American Civil Rights Movement

Use the clues below to complete the crossword puzzle.

A civil rights march in 1965

Across

2 Woman known as the "mother of the civil rights movement" after refusing to give up her seat on a bus

5 A doctrine that supported racial segregation by saying "separate but ____"

7 A group of students known as the "Little Rock ____" who were the first Black students to enter Little Rock's desegregated Central High School

8 A set of laws in the South that enforced racial segregation

10 In 1964, Martin Luther King Jr. received the ____ Peace Prize for his leadership

Down

1 ____ v. Board of Education was a 1954 ruling that declared racial segregation in public schools unconstitutional

3 The practice or policy of keeping people of different races separate from each other

4 The ____ to Montgomery marches were a series of civil rights protest marches in 1965 to support voting rights

6 Dr. Martin Luther King Jr. gave his famous "I Have a Dream" speech at the ____ memorial in Washington, D.C.

9 Over 200,000 people participated in the ____ on Washington for Jobs and Freedom in 1963 to fight for civil and economic rights of Black Americans

Martin Luther King Jr. addressing crowds in Washington, D.C., 1963

Find worksheets, games, lessons & more at education.com/resources

© 2007 - 2022 Education.com

JOURNAL PAGES

Pillar: Leading

EMPLOYEE OR COMMUNITY CITIZEN ACTIVITIES

Pillar: Leading

Leading Social Change

LESSON VOCABULARY WORDS

INSTRUCTIONS: Study the vocabulary words listed below for a good understanding of each one.

1. **Social movement**- an organized effort by a large number of people to bring about or impede social, political, economic, or cultural change. There are five types of social movements.
2. **Reform movement**- a movement that seeks some sort of change to some aspect of a nation's political, economic, or social systems. The goal is to improve conditions within the nation's current regime, not overthrow it.
3. **Self-help movements**- a movement that involves people trying to improve aspects of their personal lives; examples of self-help groups include Alcoholics Anonymous and Weight Watchers.
4. **Religious movements**- a movement started to reinforce religious beliefs among their members and to convert other people to these beliefs.
5. **Reactionary movement**- a movement initiated to block social change or to reverse social changes that have already been achieved.
6. **Revolutionary movement**- a movement that wants to replace already existing orders with a totally different structure

Activity: Watch the video and research your assigned social movement.

1. The Glass Ceiling (The Glass Ceiling by Parity.org - YouTube)
2. Voter's Suppression (Voter Suppression: It's the American Way - YouTube / Voter suppression - YouTube)
3. LGBT Movement (Wanda Sykes Takes Us Through the History of LGBTQ+ — Now You Know - YouTube)
4. Gender Pay Gap (How Iceland is Fighting the Gender Pay Gap - BBC Stories - YouTube)
5. Racism in America (Oprah Winfrey: Racism over when we release fear - Bing video)

On the chart paper provided, answer the following questions:

1) When did the movement start?
2) What was the cause of the movement?
3) Explain the importance of youth involvement within the movement.
    a) Were there any youth leaders in the movement?
    b) What role did they play?
    c) Any concrete examples?

SOCIAL MOVEMENTS

1. **Women's Movement**: The feminist movement (also known as the women's movement, or feminism) refers to a series of social movements and Political campaigns for radical and liberal reforms on women's issues created by the inequality between men and women.
2. **Disability Rights Movement**: a global movement that advocates for and secures equal rights and opportunities for people who have disabilities. In the United States, and around the world, the movement has been successful in changing laws and social attitudes to make societies more inclusive.
3. **LGBT Movement**: Lesbian, gay, bisexual, and transgender (LGBT) movements are social movements that advocate for LGBT people in society. Some focus on equal rights, such as the ongoing movement for same-sex marriage, while others focus on liberation, as in the gay liberation movement of the 1960s and 1970s.
4. **Environmental Movement**: (sometimes referred to as the ecology movement) is a diverse philosophical, social, and political movement for addressing environmental issues.
5. **Labor Movement**: consists of two main wings: the trade union movement (British English) or labor union movement (American English) on the one hand, and the political labor movement on the other. Consists of the collective organization of working people developed to represent and campaign for better working conditions and treatment from their employers and, by the implementation of labor and employment laws, from their governments. The standard unit of organization is the trade union. A political party that represents the interests of employees.
6. **Reproductive Justice Movement**: is the human right to maintain personal bodily autonomy, have children, not have children, and parent the children we have in safe and sustainable communities. The reproductive justice framework encompasses a wide range of issues affecting the reproductive lives of marginalized women, including access to: contraception, comprehensive sex education, prevention and care for sexually transmitted infections, alternative birth options, adequate prenatal and pregnancy care, domestic violence assistance, adequate wages to support families, and safe homes.
7. **Anti-War Movement**: is a social movement, usually in opposition to a particular nation's decision to start or carry on an armed conflict, unconditional of a maybe-existing just cause. It is also the opposition to all use of military force during conflicts, or to anti-war books, paintings, and other works of art.

Social Movement Questions

1. What are some issues in your community that you would like to address, change and/or improve?
   _____
   _____

2. How would you go about addressing those issues? How can you have a positive impact on your community?
   _____
   _____

JOURNAL PAGES

Pillar: Leading

Week 35 & 36 Activities

YOUTH ACTIVITIES

Financial Literacy

LESSON VOCABULARY WORDS

INSTRUCTIONS: Study the vocabulary words listed below for a good understanding of each one.

1. **Wants:** Things people like to have, but do not need.
2. **Needs:** Things that people must have to live.
3. **Save:** To keep your money to use later.
4. **Volunteer:** A person who works for no pay to help others.
5. **Tax:** A compulsory contribution to state revenue, levied by the government on workers' income and business profits, or added to the cost of some goods, services, and transactions.
6. **Tip:** A sum of money given to someone as a reward for their service.
7. **Credit score:** A number assigned to a person that indicates to lenders their capacity to repay a loan.
8. **Living wage:** A wage that is high enough to maintain a normal standard of living.

Pillar: Leading

NEEDS AND WANTS
Story By: Andrew Frinkle

"*What is success?*" Mr. Gruber asked his 6th grade business class. It was his opening conversation for the first class of the semester. "*Success is rolling in a sweet car, watching an 80-inch TV, and living in a place with at least twelve rooms.*" One student answered, earning a chorus of laughter.

Mr. Gruber smiled but shook his head. "*Tom, that is excess. That is not success.*" "*How about being able to provide for your family?*" A blonde girl named Sandy in the front suggested as an answer. "*Now we're getting closer,*" Mr. Gruber smiled, "*but try thinking about it in terms of what you need and what you want.*" "*Getting everything you want.*" Tom shouted out an answer again, trying for more laughs. Mr. Gruber sighed. "*I believe we've already talked about excess versus success.*" "*Getting everything you need, but some of what you want?*" James, sitting in the back, wondered aloud.

"*Exactly!*" Mr. Gruber clapped. "*Success is getting everything you need and some of what you want. The more you get that you want, the more successful you are. You do reach a point where you are living in excess, though.*" "*What does this have to do with business?*" Tom demanded. It seemed if it wasn't funny, he wasn't happy.

"*Well, Tom, think of it this way: the point of business is to make a living to support your family. Once you have properly seen to their needs, you can then see to getting the extras that you want.*" "*What if I don't have a family?*" He continued to be difficult. "*Then you have to provide for yourself, a family of one.*" "*He has goldfish to think about!*" Peter, Tom's friend, shouted out. "*Then he needs to provide for a family of one with a fishbowl.*" Mr. Gruber corrected himself. Tom nodded, satisfied with that answer.

"*So, in the next nine weeks, we're going to study basic business situations, like having a checking account, balancing household budgets, and understanding credit cards.*" Tom rubbed his hands together excitedly. "*When do we get to start spending?*" "*You already are, Tom. You're spending time with us!*" Mr. Gruber laughed. "*Now, let's see what you guys know about credit cards…*"

INSTRUCTIONS: Use the information in the "*Needs vs Wants*" story to answer the questions below. (Circle the correct answer.)

1. What class does Mr. Gruber teach?
    a. history
    b. science
    c. math
    d. business
2. What is the main point of this discussion?
    a. Get what you want
    a. Wants vs. Needs
    b. Money
    c. How to play the stock market
3. Which student doesn't seem to be taking the class seriously?
    a. Tom
    b. James
    c. Peter
    d. Sandy
4. How does Mr. Gruber try to keep the students interested?
    a. He is showing a movie.
    b. He is giving a lecture where only he talks.
    c. He is involving the students in a discussion.
    d. He is reading from a textbook.
5. Based on the story, how could you NOT describe Mr. Gruber?
    a. patient
    b. humorous
    c. involved
    d. grumpy

Pillar: Leading

A need is something you have to have to live.

A want is something you would like to have, but can live without.

Needs

Wants

INSTRUCTIONS: Write the name of each picture (from the list below) in the box provided above that identifies it as a need or a want.

ice cream	house	bike	toothpaste	pet
dinner	necklace	clothes	football	medicine

LIVEWORKSHEETS

THE BIGGEST LOOSER
FINANCIAL LITERARY ACTIVITY

This is a financial literacy game to help the participants to understand the necessity of being financially responsible with their money.

Materials: Play Money (dollars of all denominations and coins)
Instructions: Facilitator/Mentor will give each participant $200 and instruct them they will have to apply for more money if they run out of money or borrow it from a friend or family member.

Read the following: Tonya and Brian are starting new jobs on Monday and they both need to prepare for their first day. Tonya needs a pair of work shoes, khaki pants and some socks or footies. Brian needs a tie, some khaki pants and a belt. (The girls will buy as if they are Tanya and the boys will buy as if they are Brian.) The following are the stores closest to them to purchase their items from: Goodwill, Target, Macy's, Shoe Carnival and/or Finish Line. The following is the price list for each store:

Goodwill Store:
1. Female Work Shoes..................$12.00
2. Male Work Shoes......................$15.00
3. Khaki Pants - Female..................$10.00
4. Khaki Pants - Male....................$13.00
5. Belts...$5.00
6. Ties..$2.00
7. Polo Shirts - Female.................$7.00
8. Polo Shirts - Male....................$9.00

Target:
1. Female Work Shoes....................$34.99
2. Male Work Shoes........................$39.99
3. Khaki Pants - Female..................$15.99
4. Khaki Pants - Male......................$18.99
5. Belts...$12.99
6. Ties..$6.99
7. Polo Shirts - Female.................$14.99
8. Polo Shirts - Male....................$15.99

Macy's (All popular name brand items):
1. Female Work Shoes....................$49.99
2. Male Work Shoes........................$65.99
3. Khaki Pants - Female..................$24.99
4. Khaki Pants - Male......................$29.99
5. Belts...$15.99
6. Ties..$9.99
7. Polo Shirts - Female.................$19.99
8. Polo Shirts - Male....................$21.99

Shoe Carnival:
1. Female Work Shoes (Timberlands)..............$59.99
2. Male Work Shoes (Timberlands)..................$64.99
3. Belts..$14.99

Finish Line:
1. Female Work Shoes (Nlke)..........................$34.99
2. Male Work Shoes (Nike)..............................$54.99
3. Belts (Name Brand)...................................$9.99
4. Polo Shirts - Female (Name Brand)............$12.99
5. Polo Shirts - Male (Name Brand)................$16.99

Have each participant decide where they will shop and make their selections. They are to deduct the amount spent from their money on hand ($200). Once they have made their selections, give money to the Facilitator/Mentor, who will act as the bank (if actualy play money is used). Note: Banker refuse all loan requests as applicant hasn't been on their job long enough and there isn't a guarantee of repayment.

Instruct the participants they have added expenses that they will have to deduct from their money:
1. Two week bus pass...................$25.00
2. Lunch for two weeks
   a. Purchasing lunch items from store: ..$25.00 (carrying lunch to work)
   b. Eating at the food court daily..........$50.00

If they do not have enough money for the additional expenses they will have to apply for a loan at the bank or borrow the money from a family member or friend.
Have participants count how much money they have left over to put into their rainy day fund savings account.
Whoever has the most money left will have their money doubled to go shopping for more needed items or to save.
The next highest will receive an additional 75% of their remaining money to go shopping for more needed items or to save.
The third highest will receive an additional 50% of their remaining money to go shopping for more needed items or to save.
The fourth highest will receive an addition 25% of their remaining money to go shopping for more needed items or to save.
If there is anyone who had to borrow from the bank, friend or family member. They will not receive any additional funds and will be seen as the biggest loser.

EMPLOYEE OR COMMUNITY CITIZEN ACTIVITIES

Financial Literacy

LESSON VOCABULARY WORDS

INSTRUCTIONS: Review vocabulary words listed below with the participants to ensure they have a good understanding of each before starting any of the activities.

1. **Wants:** Things people like to have, but do not need.
2. **Needs:** Things that people must have to live.
3. **Save:** To keep your money to use later.
4. **Volunteer:** A person who works for no pay to help others.
5. **Tax:** A compulsory contribution to state revenue, levied by the government on workers' income and business profits, or added to the cost of some goods, services, and transactions.
6. **Tip:** A sum of money given to someone as a reward for their service.
7. **Credit score:** A number assigned to a person that indicates to lenders their capacity to repay a loan.
8. **Living wage:** A wage that is high enough to maintain a normal standard of living.

Pillar: Leading

Name: _____

Needs and Wants

Directions: Categorize the list of words below into what a person **needs** to survive, and what a person **wants** to have in his or her life.

```
food      bicycle     ice cream     air      television    water
shelter   cell phone  clothing      family   toys
games     bed         music         trees    electricity   shoes
```

Directions: Discuss your choices with a partner. Are there any choices you made with which your partner disagrees? Explain your choices.

© www.HaveFunTeaching.com

HOW TO MAKE A BUDGET

Surprises are nice, but not when it comes to your money. If you're scrambling to pay the bills each month, you would probably benefit from having a budget. Below are three methods for helping you organize and manage your monthly expenses.

FIXED AND FLEX

The first budgeting technique involves grouping your expenses into two categories—"fixed," which are must-haves like food and utilities, and "flex," the nice-to-haves like a new watch or a day at the spa. Keeping these definitions in mind, follow the four-step process below:

- ☐ Gather 6 to 12 months of bank statements, receipts, and other financial records.
- ☐ Separate those expenses into "Fixed" and "Flex" columns.
- ☐ Add up your monthly "Fixed" expenses, then subtract the total from your monthly income.
- ☐ What's left over is your "Flex" spending money.

Although you're still dealing with the same amount of money, looking at your finances in a more organized way can help get your spending under control.

THE 50/30/20 RULE

Another budgeting technique is the 50/30/20 rule. It involves dividing your monthly income into three "buckets":

- ☐ 50% (or less) goes to necessities such as housing, student loans, and utilities. These are expenses you have to pay every month.
- ☐ 30% (or less) goes to nice-to-haves, such as entertainment, hobbies, and travel.
- ☐ 20% (or more, if possible) goes toward savings and paying down debt.

You can adjust the 50/30/20 rule based on your short- and long-term goals but be careful about confusing "nice-to-haves" for "necessities." Several dinners out each week and unlimited data plans may be nice to have, but they aren't essential.

TRACKING

Tracking takes the most time, but it provides the greatest insight into your spending habits.

- ☐ Use a spreadsheet, an online service or, if you prefer to go "low tech," a notebook and pen will work just fine.
- ☐ First, create columns for your spending categories (e.g., groceries, gas, utilities, medical, entertainment, and childcare). Add a "miscellaneous/unexpected" and a "savings" category, as well.
- ☐ Next, divide your monthly income among the categories and then pay your bills/save accordingly. It's important to list all items and subtract the amount you spend in each category, so you know where your money is going. Once a category is "out of money":
- ☐ Stop spending in that category, if possible, until you get your next paycheck
- ☐ Consider making trade-offs by moving money around from other categories

Pillar: Leading

You stretch your money in many directions. Daily expenses, entertainment, life events, and long-term goals all compete for the same dollar. Budgeting can help ensure you're covering the necessary monthly expenses, saving for the future, and—maybe—have some extra cash to reward yourself for your good work. (https://www.tiaa.org/public/learn/personal-finance-101/how-to-make-a-budget)

EXPENSE TRACKER

DATE	DESCRIPTION	AMOUNT SPENT	CASH	CREDIT	NEED	WANT
			☐	☐	☐	☐
			☐	☐	☐	☐
			☐	☐	☐	☐
			☐	☐	☐	☐
			☐	☐	☐	☐
			☐	☐	☐	☐
			☐	☐	☐	☐
			☐	☐	☐	☐
			☐	☐	☐	☐
			☐	☐	☐	☐
			☐	☐	☐	☐
			☐	☐	☐	☐
			☐	☐	☐	☐
			☐	☐	☐	☐
			☐	☐	☐	☐
			☐	☐	☐	☐
			☐	☐	☐	☐
			☐	☐	☐	☐
			☐	☐	☐	☐
			☐	☐	☐	☐
			☐	☐	☐	☐

www.ShiningMom.com

Pillar: Leading

Name: _____

Needs and Wants

Directions: Categorize the list of words below into what a person **needs** to survive, and what a person **wants** to have in his or her life.

food	bicycle	ice cream	air	television	water
shelter	cell phone	clothing		family	toys
games	bed	music	trees	electricity	shoes

Directions: Discuss your choices with a partner. Are there any choices you made with which your partner disagrees? Explain your choices.

© www.HaveFunTeaching.com

THE BIGGEST LOOSER
FINANCIAL LITERARY ACTIVITY

This is a financial literacy game to help the participants to understand the necessity of being financially responsible with their money.

Materials: Play Money (dollars of all denominations and coins)

Instructions: Facilitator/Mentor will give each participant $200 and instruct them they will have to apply for more money if they run out of money or borrow it from a friend or family member.

Read the following: Tonya and Brian are starting new jobs on Monday and they both need to prepare for their first day. Tonya needs a pair of work shoes, khaki pants and some socks or footies. Brian needs a tie, some khaki pants and a belt. (The girls will buy as if they are Tanya and the boys will buy as if they are Brian.) The following are the stores closest to them to purchase their items from: Goodwill, Target, Macy's, Shoe Carnival and/or Finish Line. The following is the price list for each store:

Goodwill Store:
1. Female Work Shoes.................$12.00
2. Male Work Shoes....................$15.00
3. Khaki Pants - Female...............$10.00
4. Khaki Pants - Male..................$13.00
5. Belts...$5.00
6. Ties..$2.00
7. Polo Shirts - Female................$7.00
8. Polo Shirts - Male...................$9.00

Target:
1. Female Work Shoes.................$34.99
2. Male Work Shoes....................$39.99
3. Khaki Pants - Female...............$15.99
4. Khaki Pants - Male..................$18.99
5. Belts.......................................$12.99
6. Ties..$6.99
7. Polo Shirts - Female...............$14.99
8. Polo Shirts - Male..................$15.99

Macy's (All popular name brand items):
1. Female Work Shoes.................$49.99
2. Male Work Shoes....................$65.99
3. Khaki Pants - Female...............$24.99
4. Khaki Pants - Male..................$29.99
5. Belts.......................................$15.99
6. Ties..$9.99
7. Polo Shirts - Female...............$19.99
8. Polo Shirts - Male..................$21.99

Shoe Carnival:
1. Female Work Shoes (Timberlands)..............$59.99
2. Male Work Shoes (Timberlands).................$64.99
3. Belts..$14.99

Finish Line:
1. Female Work Shoes (NIke)........................$34.99
2. Male Work Shoes (Nike)...........................$54.99
3. Belts (Name Brand)..................................$9.99
4. Polo Shirts - Female (Name Brand)...........$12.99
5. Polo Shirts - Male (Name Brand)...............$16.99

Have each participant decide where they will shop and make their selections. They are to deduct the amount spent from their money on hand ($200). Once they have made their selections, give money to the Facilitator/Mentor, who will act as the bank (if actualy play money is used). Note: Banker refuse all loan requests as applicant hasn't been on their job long enough and there isn't a guarantee of repayment.

Instruct the participants they have added expenses that they will have to deduct from their money:
1. Two week bus pass..................................$25.00
2. Lunch for two weeks
   a. Purchasing lunch items from store: ..$25.00 (carrying lunch to work)
   b. Eating at the food court daily..........$50.00

If they do not have enough money for the additional expenses they will have to apply for a loan at the bank or borrow the money from a family member or friend.

Have participants count how much money they have left over to put into their rainy day fund savings account.

Whoever has the most money left will have their money doubled to go shopping for more needed items or to save.
The next highest will receive an additional 75% of their remaining money to go shopping for more needed items or to save.
The third highest will receive an additional 50% of their remaining money to go shopping for more needed items or to save.
The fourth highest will receive an addition 25% of their remaining money to go shopping for more needed items or to save.
If there is anyone who had to borrow from the bank, friend or family member. They will not receive any additional funds and will be seen as the biggest loser.

Week 37 & 38 Activities

YOUTH ACTIVITIES

Pillar: Leading

Character Development

LESSON VOCABULARY WORDS

INSTRUCTIONS: Study the vocabulary words listed below for a good understanding of each one.

1. **Character Trait:** a way to describe someone.
2. **Character:** how your habits, motives, thoughts, and so on relate to morality, particularly as it concerns integrity.
3. **Values:** the things that you believe are important in the way you live and work.
4. **Mentor:** An experienced and trusted advisor.
5. **Transformation:** A thorough or dramatic change in form or appearance.

There are many factors that influence our character. Some of those factors are beyond our control while others play a role in molding our character. Regardless, the greatest influence on a person's character is that which we have ultimate power over how we respond to the circumstances. The following are some character traits to consider:

Generosity: seeing what others need and giving my resources to help them.

Adaptability: eagerly embracing a change in plans without complaint.

Cooperation: finding ways to understand others and work together to achieve a goal.

Courage: confidently doing what is right even if I feel afraid.

Creativity: approaching a need, task, or idea from a unique or new perspective.

Decisiveness: resolving a tough choice by evaluating what will achieve the greatest good.

Dependability: building trust with others by doing what I say I will do.

Diligence: pursuing a task until it is finished.

Endurance: using my inward strength to accomplish what is difficult even when I feel like giving up.

Forgiveness: clearing the record of someone who has wronged me and showing them love instead.

Truthfulness: speaking only what is honest and factual.

Self-Control: choosing to do what is right when I feel like doing wrong.

There are more identified character traits than what is listed. Feel free to check them out on your own and/or when completing the activity. (https://www.craftionary.net/character-trait-crafts-activities-kids/)

Activity: Create a comic strip showing how you define character.

Comic Strip

JOURNAL PAGES

Pillar: Leading

EMPLOYEE OR COMMUNITY CITIZEN ACTIVITIES

Pillar: Leading

Character Development

LESSON VOCABULARY WORDS

INSTRUCTIONS: Study the vocabulary words listed below for a good understanding of each one.

1. **Adolescence:** The period following the onset of puberty during which a young person develops from a child into an adult.
2. **Maturity:** The state, fact, or period of being mature.
3. **Transformation:** A thorough or dramatic change in form or appearance.

CHARACTER TRAITS

While there are many character traits that can contribute to career success, here are some of the top characteristics that can help you advance in a community setting or the workplace:

a. **Ambitious.** A strong desire to achieve success by meeting their goals and applied hard work and dedication to overcome a challenge or exceed goals/objectives.
b. **Creative.** Uses their imagination to make or invent something and is applicable when solving a difficult problem, presenting information in a clear, interesting way or finding better ways to complete tasks.
c. **Compassionate.** Someone who can both feel and express sympathy for others.
d. **Conscientious.** Someone who is careful and takes purposeful action and concerned with doing what is right to fulfill a duty.
e. **Courageous.** Someone who is not deterred by challenges and difficulties, takes calculated risks, and takes on projects others fear may be too hard or require too much work.
f. **Flexible.** Can quickly adapt to changes in plans and is critical to succeeding in various roles.
g. **Honest.** Someone who is sincere, honest, and generally does not feel comfortable participating in deceptive practices.
h. **Humble.** Someone who exercises humility, are respectful, and displays leadership traits.
i. **Honorable** (Integrity). Someone who acts according to their principles and ethics.
j. **Loyal.** Someone who is supportive and trustworthy.
k. **Patient.** Someone who can tolerate setbacks, delays, or unexpected challenges without becoming anxious or angry.
l. **Persistent.** Someone who is relentless in the pursuit of goals and continues along their path despite any obstacles or difficulties they may face.
m. **Resilient.** Someone who can quickly recover from setbacks, stress, adverse situations, or unexpected changes.
n. **Disciplined.** Someone who can overcome temptations, procrastination, and self-doubt.
o. **Curious.** Someone with the drive to want to know or learn new skills, information, and abilities strategically and with motivation.

These positive character traits are examples of sought-after personality and behaviors. Understanding your best and most relevant character traits can also support setting and attaining goals.

Activity: Make a list of 4 to 6 character traits that you intend to exemplify (words you believe describe who you are striving to become). During discussion time, share your list of "core values" and why you selected those core values.

Core Value	Explanation why you chose this core value.

Promises, Promises Activity: write out some promises you made to your younger self. Make a list of them and be sure and include some you failed to keep. Next, select one of those unkept promises (to yourself or to someone else), and determine to keep that promise for one whole week. Write it down and think of the steps you can take to keep that promise to yourself. Choose an accountability partner who will hold you accountable, encourage and inspire you to continue working to attain this goal. During the next week's session, share the goal you selected and your progress in honoring it for a week. What has it meant to you to keep this promise? How did it positively impact or affect your character? Did it strengthen your discipline?

_____
_____
_____
_____
_____
_____
_____
_____
_____

Pillar: Leading

Current Events Activity: Watch the news and look for news stories about people who either exhibited strong character (integrity and ethics) or failed to do so. Write out a summary of what you think made them act the way they did. In your summary, include what values they demonstrated (or did not demonstrate): self-centered, self-promoting and self-protecting or civic-minded, others-centered and/or self-sacrificing.

_____
_____
_____
_____
_____
_____
_____
_____
_____
_____

I had to See it to Believe it Activity: Observe your co-workers in your workplace. Look for instances where men or women either exhibit strong character (integrity and ethics) or failed to do so. Write out a summary of what positive/negative character traits you witnessed and why you think they behaved in that manner. Be honest in your interpretation of the individual's character traits. In your summary, include what values they demonstrated (or did not demonstrate): self-centered, self-promoting and self-protecting or civic-minded, others-centered and/or self-sacrificing.

_____
_____
_____
_____
_____
_____
_____
_____
_____
_____

Lesson Summary: Explain, in written form, how positive character traits are displayed in everyday life, the workplace, and the community. Be prepared to share during your discussion time.

_____
_____
_____
_____
_____
_____
_____
_____

Discussion Questions:

1. What does it mean to have good character?

   _____
   _____
   _____

2. Identify five people who you respect and admire in your personal and/or professional life? Share what you respect and admire about them. Identify which positive character traits you have seen in them.

   _____
   _____
   _____

3. What could someone do that would make you no longer respect or admire them?

   _____
   _____

Your reputation is what others think of you; your character is who you truly are. Reputations can be manipulated; character can only be developed and maintained.

JOURNAL PAGES

Pillar: Leading

Pillar: Leading

Week 39 & 40 Activities

YOUTH ACTIVITIES

Lead by Example

LESSON VOCABULARY WORDS

INSTRUCTIONS: Study the vocabulary words listed below for a good understanding of each one.

1. **Leadership**: The action of leading a group of people or an organization.

2. **Example**: A thing or characteristic of its kind or illustrating a general rule.

3. **Impact**: The effect or influence of one person, thing, or action, on another.

4. **Guidance**: Advice or information aimed at resolving a problem or difficulty, especially as given by someone in authority.

Discussion Questions:

1. What does it mean to be a leader/influencer?

   _____
   _____
   _____
   _____

2. Do you see yourself as a leader/influencer?

   _____
   _____
   _____
   _____

3. Name one leader in your family, and one at your school.

   a. _____
   b. _____

Pillar: Leading

4. Is it hard for you to admit to your mistakes? Why or why not?

   _____
   _____
   _____

5. Who should not become a leader and lead people? Can everyone become a leader?

   _____
   _____
   _____

6. From the video, how important is it to work and collaborate with others?

   _____
   _____
   _____
   _____

7. Discussion questions: How can someone be a leader even at home, while a lot of participants are learning virtually?

   _____
   _____
   _____

8. Have you demonstrated any leadership qualities since the last meeting?

   _____
   _____
   _____

Reflection: Leaders are not perfect, but they seek to build trust when working with others. They learn how to be responsible and admit when they've made a mistake. Being a leader does not mean you are superhuman.

JOURNAL PAGES

Pillar: Leading

EMPLOYEE OR COMMUNITY CITIZEN ACTIVITIES

Intentional Mentoring Mentee's Workbook

LESSON VOCABULARY WORDS

INSTRUCTIONS: Study the vocabulary words listed below for a good understanding of each one.

1. **Leadership:** The action of leading a group of people or an organization.

2. **Example:** A thing or characteristic of its kind or illustrating a general rule.

3. **Impact**: The effect or influence of one person, thing, or action, on another.

4. **Guidance:** Advice or information aimed at resolving a problem or difficulty, especially as given by someone in authority.

_____
_____
_____
_____
_____
_____
_____

Discussion Topic: *"Collaboration captures collective intelligence. Coming together is a beginning. Keeping together is progress. Working together is success."* – Unknown

Why is it important to NOT lead with a *"Do as I say, not as I do"* approach?

_____
_____
_____
_____
_____
_____
_____

Pillar: Leading

Discussion Questions:

1. Do you consider yourself a leader?

2. What does it mean to be a leader?

3. Name one leader in your family, and one at your community.

   a. _____

   b. _____

4. Is it hard for you to admit to your mistakes? Why or why not?

5. Who should not become a leader and lead people? Can everyone become a leader?

6. Discussion questions: How can someone be a leader even at home, while a lot of participants are learning virtually?

_____

_____

_____

7. Have you demonstrated any leadership qualities since the last meeting?

_____

_____

_____

Pillar: Leading

THE LEADER IN ME SELF EVALUATION

INSTRUCTIONS: Circle the smiley face that closely represents the truthfulness of the statement.

Habit 1: Be Proactive

1. I am responsible	☹ 😐 🙂
2. I take initiative	☹ 😐 🙂
3. I have a good attitude most of the time	☹ 😐 🙂
4. I make good choices	☹ 😐 🙂
5. I do the right thing without being asked	☹ 😐 🙂

Habit 2: Begin with the End in Mind

1. I plan ahead	☹ 😐 🙂
2. I set goals	☹ 😐 🙂
3. I am a good citizen	☹ 😐 🙂
4. I contribute to my school's mission/vision	☹ 😐 🙂

Habit 3: Put First Things First

1. I set priorities	☹ 😐 🙂
2. I am organized	☹ 😐 🙂
3. I am disciplined	☹ 😐 🙂

https://www.pinterest.com/pin/26037122269545288/

TWO ACTIVITIES THAT SHOWCASE DIFFERENT LEADERSHIP STYLES

There are three different 'leadership styles.' These are: **autocratic** (also known as authoritarian), **delegative** (also called 'free reign)' and **democratic** (which is also called participative) (Clark, 2015; Johnson-Gerard, 2017).

An ***autocratic leader*** makes decisions without first consulting others, while a ***delegative leader*** allows the staff to make the decisions (Johnson-Gerard, 2017). Finally, a ***democratic leader*** consults with the staff in making workplace decisions (Johnson-Gerard, 2017). Here is an excellent resource for exploring different leadership styles. The workbook also provides some helpful worksheets. The following two activities help participants think more deeply about styles of leadership. The group should be divided into small groups of 3 – 4 participants. The participants work in groups for the first activity, and then they work individually on the second activity.

ACTIVITY ONE (Clark, 2015)

As a group or with your mentor, determine which leadership style is used in the following scenario: *"A new supervisor has just been put in charge of the production line. He immediately starts by telling the crew what change needs to be made. When some suggestions are made, he tells them he does not have time to consider them."* Put yourself in this or a similar situation and determine what your reaction is to the leadership style discussed.

ACTIVITY TWO (Clark, 2015)

Statement: *"Consider a time when you, or another leader, used the authoritarian (autocratic), participative (democratic) or delegative (free reign) style of leadership."* Answer the following questions:

a. Was it effective?

_____

_____

b. Would a different leadership style have worked better?

_____

_____

c. What were the employees' experiences?

_____

_____

d. What did they learn from the leadership style?

_____

_____

e. What did they learn?

Pillar: Leading

f. Which style is easiest to use (and why)?

g. Which style which the participant prefers (and why).

DISCUSSION TOPIC: What did you learn about the three styles of leadership.

7 KEYS TO CREATIVE COLLABORATION

INSTRUCTIONS: How it can the following be used in your life and/or business:

1. **Ownership**: Members need to be empowered from the start.

2. **Dependability**: Creative collaboration requires members to hit their deadlines and develop creative endurance.

3. **Trust**: When members trust one another, they work interdependently and genuinely listen to one another and assume the best in each other. Over time, they become transparent and even vulnerable.

4. **Structure**: The structure should be loose and flexible. But you need to have structure in creative collaboration.

5. **A Shared Vision**: This isn't conducive to a vision statement. Its more like of a sense of direction. A shared desire, a goal you are aiming for, and picture of what you will produce.

6. **Fun**: The best collaborative groups are the ones where you want to be together, laugh and work towards a shared vision. It boosts both convergent thinking and divergent thinking.

7. **Candor**: It's the idea that groups need to be honest about what's working and failing. This honesty allows you to adjust and iterate and ultimately create something awesome.

8. **Propose a scenario** What if you were working on a group project, and you were the only person that did any work, how would you respond? Allow your creativity to inspire you to come up with workable scenarios. (https://www.youtube.com/watch?v=VmQVNE-MbKI)

JOURNAL PAGES

> "LEADERS DON'T CREATE FOLLOWERS, THEY CREATE MORE LEADERS."
> - TOM PETERS

Pillar: Leading

PILLAR: LEGACY

PILLAR: LEGACY

"Living your legacy is one of the best ways to feel happy while you journey through life."
– Shyam Ramanathan

In the previous pillars, you have discovered the importance of living, loving, learning, laughing, and leading. All of which are necessary for you to live the legacy you want to leave the world NOW. Benjamin Franklin once said, *"Don't put off until tomorrow what you can do today."* Living your legacy is one of the greatest gifts you can give to yourself, your family, the community, and the world all at the same time. I know what you may think, *how can I do that*? The information in this pillar will hopefully help you begin your journey of living the legacy you desire to leave the world. Yep, it begins with understanding, accepting, and believing what legacy is. Legacy is a living reflection of who you are. It is your story, unfolding in real time, and inspired by what makes life fulfilling.

Understanding what living your legacy entails begins with learning what is legacy life, eulogy and resume values are. This basic understanding will begin the journey you are now on even though you haven't decided to live a life of legacy. As Maya Angelo said, *"…when you know better, do better."*

- **Legacy Life**: is a life that has a positive impact on someone else; makes conscious decisions each day; consciously focuses on the NOW moments that occur in life; happily, shares their time, attention, and essence with the ones they love and encounter daily; and spends time developing and completing their legacy life goals.

- **Eulogy Values**: are what makes you stand for your highest values and by your deepest convictions; gives you the big picture of your life and gives you the impetus to create the life you desire. It is the virtues that show your inner light and inner character.

- **Resume Values**: are the results of a life lived for external achievement. They are the skills and strategies you need for career success and build an external career that results in you living with an unconscious boredom, separated from the deepest meaning of life and highest moral joys.

BE ENTHUSIASTIC:

Get excited about your life! This is your opportunity to experience this world as it is. Genuine happiness draws others to you and allows you to build trusting and long-lasting relationships. Enthusiasm unlocks a life of substance and cheer; and be enthusiastic about life despite the obstacles each one faces.

BE GRATEFUL

Your attitude towards everything in life plays a greater role in how you like life and the opportunities you go after. Develop coping skills to view the world through a prism of abundance. Your attitude is the accurate barometer of how you experience your life. Your attitude sets the temperature for how other people see, relate, trust, and treat you. It can attract abundance and joy. When you're grateful your life has the ability to bring joy. The joy you experience while living your legacy is not based upon your outer success but your internal happiness. His/Her gratefulness is developed one small appreciative moment at a time. So, savor them and revere life.

ACCEPT YOURSELF

In the pillar on living, we talked about discovering what you like, what you are passionate about. Identify those things you believe will bring you happiness and/or the drive you use to live your best life now. By doing so, this will help you live "...*thriving, vibrant, happy 'lives'.*" This gives you permission to live life well by doing things today that help you flourish in the moment, and in every day thereafter. Because this isn't something that is taught in the school or in some cultures, where it is socially acceptable. It must be introduced as an acceptable part of life for people to explore its necessity in their life.

Remember, your life is a gift! Accept the gift you have been given as the greatest present you have ever received. Live it by honoring it in the ways you talk about you, the love you lavish on it daily and the respect you freely give and receive. You are unique, no one else is equipped to be you. When you were created, the mold was broken. In an interview, Oprah Winfrey did in 2015, she shares "*What Mispronouncing 'Canada' on TV*" taught her. It taught her to always be who she is and show the essence of her truth. Otherwise, you will not be seen as being genuine. Accept the uniqueness that is you and live the legacy you want to leave your family, community, and world. Activate your gifts and talents and tap into your amazing strengths. If you don't do it, it will never be done. In the same way, you are not equipped to be anyone else.

Pillar: Legacy

"You have no idea what your legacy will be. Your legacy is what you do every day. Your legacy is every life you've touched, every person whose life was either moved or not. It's every person you've harmed or helped. That's your legacy." – Maya Angelou

CHARACTER: is the mental and moral qualities distinctive to an individual; strength and originality in a person's nature; a person's excellent reputation.

CHARACTER

Live your life according to your core values. Think about it this way: keep the end in mind and align all your activities to your highest values. Align your actions to what you want your life to stand for to ensure you live your legacy.

INSPIRE OTHERS

The way to inspire others is by being an influencer. One of the side effects of being a leader is inspiring others to tap into the best version of themselves and LIVE! In most cases, simply showing up as your authentic self enables, inspires, and empowers others to do the same.

ALWAYS RESPECT OTHERS

Live your life with one undeniable truth: respect is inherent! It shows that you value others as much as you value the gift that you are to the world. With that as a core value, always respect others. It frees you to continue living your best life while silently giving others permission to do the same.

DESERVING SUCCESS

Take positive action to overcome whatever fears you have developed over the years. It speaks to your self-love, acceptance, and the respect you have for yourself. Living your legacy means taking advantage of the opportunities available to you with the mindset that you are deserving of success. This is a tool to help you experience the success you desire. Believing in yourself means you believe you deserve success, and by acting out that belief daily, you put yourself in alignment with experiencing the success you want and deserve.

In the article, *Enlist In Your Purpose: Live Your Legacy Now*, author, Heather Burgett, suggests each person seeking to live their legacy now should:

- ✓ Thrive through uncertain times.
- ✓ Stop making everything about YOU.
- ✓ Tap into your signature gifts.
- ✓ Recognize your sole reason to connect, interact, engage and be here for others – leads to unexpected opportunities for success.
- ✓ Be cognizant of this core belief: how I do one thing is how I do everything.
- ✓ Be a visionary who implements steps to create and effect change.
- ✓ Use life altering moments to fuel and/or energize you.
- ✓ Stretch, grow and move through challenges and unimaginable circumstances.
- ✓ Recognize the beauty in knowing YOU have the power to connect and support others.

Week 41 & 42 Activities

YOUTH ACTIVITIES

Pillar: Legacy

Understanding Legacy

LESSON VOCABULARY WORDS

INSTRUCTIONS: Study the vocabulary words listed below for a good understanding of each one.

1. **Acceptance**: the action or process of being received as adequate or suitable, typically to be admitted into a group.

2. **Memory:** something remembered from the past; a recollection.

3. **Impact**: The effect or influence of one person, thing, or action, on another.

4. **Life Map:** a visual timeline that traces key moments in your life from the time you were born until the present day.

UNDERSTANDING LEGACY WORKSHEET

INSTRUCTIONS: Answer the following questions.

a. What is a "Legacy"?

_____
_____
_____

b. Are you working to leave a legacy within your family, community and/or the world?

_____
_____
_____

c. What does it mean to be a legacy? Explain your answer.

_____
_____
_____

d. What is the legacy journey? Explain your answer.

_____
_____
_____

e. Name one person who has a legacy. It must be someone in their family who left a legacy.

_____
_____
_____

f. What legacy can you leave behind?

_____
_____
_____

Reflection: Knowing the legacy you want to leave behind helps you stay focused on what you're doing in the present so that your goals are in line with that legacy.

Pillar: Legacy

JOURNAL PAGES

"If you are going to live, leave a legacy. Make a mark on the world that can't be erased." – Maya Angelou

Pillar: Legacy

EMPLOYEE OR COMMUNITY CITIZEN ACTIVITIES

Pillar: Legacy

Understanding Legacy

LESSON VOCABULARY WORDS

INSTRUCTIONS: Study the vocabulary words listed below for a good understanding of each one.

1. **Acceptance**: the action or process of being received as adequate or suitable, typically to be admitted into a group.

2. **Memory**: something remembered from the past; a recollection.

3. **Impact**: The effect or influence of one person, thing, or action, on another.

4. **Life Map:** a visual timeline that traces key moments in your life from the time you were born until the present day.

Intentional Mentoring Mentee's Workbook

UNDERSTANDING LEGACY WORKSHEET

INSTRUCTIONS: Answer the following questions.

a. What is a "Legacy"?

___

b. Are you working to leave a legacy within your family, community and/or the world?

___

c. What does it mean to be a legacy? Explain your answer.

___

d. What is the journey of a legacy? Explain your answer.

___

e. Name one person who has a legacy. It must be someone in their family who left a legacy.

___

f. What legacy can you leave behind?

___

JOURNAL PAGES

"Carve your name on hearts, not tombstones. A legacy is etched into the minds of others and the stories they share about you." ~ Shannon L. Addler

Pillar: Legacy

Week 43 & 44 Activities

YOUTH ACTIVITIES

Living your Legacy

LESSON VOCABULARY WORDS

INSTRUCTIONS: Study the vocabulary words listed below for a good understanding of each one.

1. **Acceptance**: the action or process of being received as adequate or suitable, typically to be admitted into a group.

2. **Memory**: something remembered from the past; a recollection.

3. **Impact**: The effect or influence of one person, thing, or action, on another.

4. **Life Map**: a visual timeline that traces key moments in your life from the time you were born until the present day.

Pillar: Legacy

LIFE MAP INSTRUCTIONS: WHAT SHOULD YOUR MAP INCLUDE?

- ☐ A symbol or picture that represents each selected event. The picture should give an indication of how you felt about the event.
- ☐ A label which identifies and roughly dates the event. You can be creative and poetic with these labels e.g. the road to happiness on my new skateboard.
- ☐ Connectors between events which help the viewer understand the order in which they happened. The connectors can also indicate how the road between one event and another event are connected. What important lesson or understanding did you come to during this period of time?
    - ■ Some people use arrows, some people draw roads, some people draw a bunch of islands and draw little boats travelling between each; it is up to you how you see your map. Does your life map have a road map, a diagram, a geographical map, a maze, a swirling circle or a game of snakes and ladders?

Sample list to motivate your life map drawing:

- ☐ Day you were born
- ☐ Stories you have heard about your birth
- ☐ Your earliest childhood memory (describe in detail)
- ☐ Your most vivid childhood experiences
- ☐ Your school years
- ☐ A special trip you have taken
- ☐ A favorite meaningful thing/object you received from someone special
- ☐ The first time you gave a speech
- ☐ The first time you wrote an essay
- ☐ A time you hurt yourself
- ☐ A very funny event
- ☐ A time when you cried
- ☐ Your first bike ride
- ☐ A memorable/favorite book
- ☐ A hospital stay
- ☐ Your first plane flight
- ☐ A day you met someone famous
- ☐ A death in the family
- ☐ Your First love
- ☐ The Day You Realized the Purpose for Life or for Your Life

Reflection of My Life...

When your Life Map is complete, answer the following questions:

- ☐ Imagine your life-map belongs to someone else. How do you feel about that person when you look at the life map?
- ☐ What values do you notice reflected in the important events?
- ☐ What would you change about your life-map if you could? Why?
- ☐ Where are you going in the future?
- ☐ List and describe 3 things you can do in your life stage now to make future life stages happen the way you'd like them to?

(https://www.iroquoiscsd.org/cms/lib/NY19000365/Centricity/Domain/79/Creating-a-life-map.ppt; https://www.edrawmind.com/how-to-create-a-life-map-with-examples.html)

Intentional Mentoring Mentee's Workbook

DRAWING A LIFE MAP

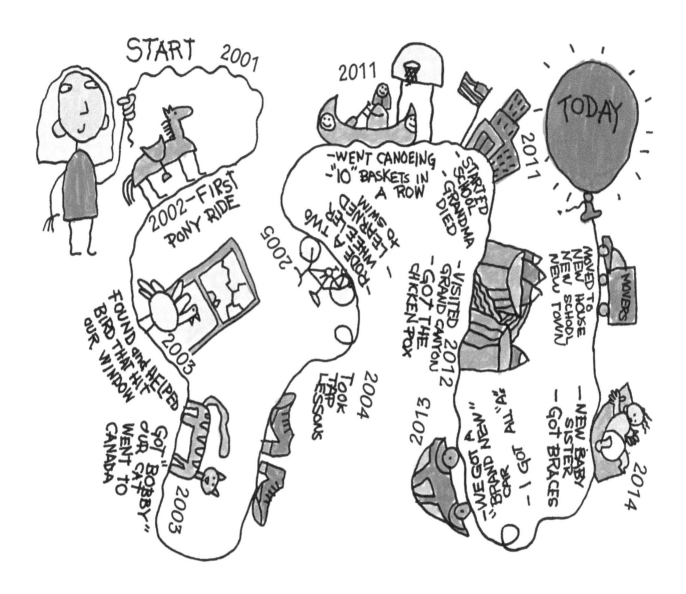

EMPLOYEE OR COMMUNITY CITIZEN ACTIVITIES

Living Your Legacy

LESSON VOCABULARY WORDS

INSTRUCTIONS: Study the vocabulary words listed below for a good understanding of each one.

1. **Acceptance**: the action or process of being received as adequate or suitable, typically to be admitted into a group.

2. **Memory:** something remembered from the past; a recollection.

3. **Impact**: The effect or influence of one person, thing, or action, on another.

4. **Life Map:** a visual timeline that traces key moments in your life from the time you were born until the present day.

Pillar: Legacy

LIFE MAP INSTRUCTIONS: WHAT SHOULD YOUR MAP INCLUDE?

- ☐ A symbol or picture that represents each selected event. The picture should give an indication of how you felt about the event.
- ☐ A label which identifies and roughly dates the event. You can be creative and poetic with these labels e.g. the road to happiness on my new skateboard.
- ☐ Connectors between events which help the viewer understand the order in which they happened. The connectors can also indicate how the road between one event and another event are connected. What important lesson or understanding did you come to during this period of time?
  - ■ Some people use arrows, some people draw roads, some people draw a bunch of islands and draw little boats travelling between each; it is up to you how you see your map. Does your life map have a road map, a diagram, a geographical map, a maze, a swirling circle or a game of snakes and ladders?

Sample list to motivate your life map drawing:

- ☐ Day you were born
- ☐ Stories you have heard about your birth
- ☐ Your earliest childhood memory (describe in detail)
- ☐ Your most vivid childhood experiences
- ☐ Your school years
- ☐ A special trip you have taken
- ☐ A favorite meaningful thing/object you received from someone special
- ☐ The first time you gave a speech
- ☐ The first time you wrote an essay
- ☐ A time you hurt yourself
- ☐ A very funny event
- ☐ A time when you cried
- ☐ Your first bike ride
- ☐ A memorable/favorite book
- ☐ A hospital stay
- ☐ Your first plane flight
- ☐ A day you met someone famous
- ☐ A death in the family
- ☐ Your First love
- ☐ The Day You Realized the Purpose for Life or for Your Life

Reflection of My Life…

When your Life Map is complete, answer the following questions:

- ☐ Imagine your life-map belongs to someone else. How do you feel about that person when you look at the life map?
- ☐ What values do you notice reflected in the important events?
- ☐ What would you change about your life-map if you could? Why?
- ☐ Where are you going in the future?
- ☐ List and describe 3 things you can do in your life stage now to make future life stages happen the way you'd like them to?

(https://www.iroquoiscsd.org/cms/lib/NY19000365/Centricity/Domain/79/Creating-a-life-map.ppt; https://www.edrawmind.com/how-to-create-a-life-map-with-examples.html)

CREATING A LIFE MAP

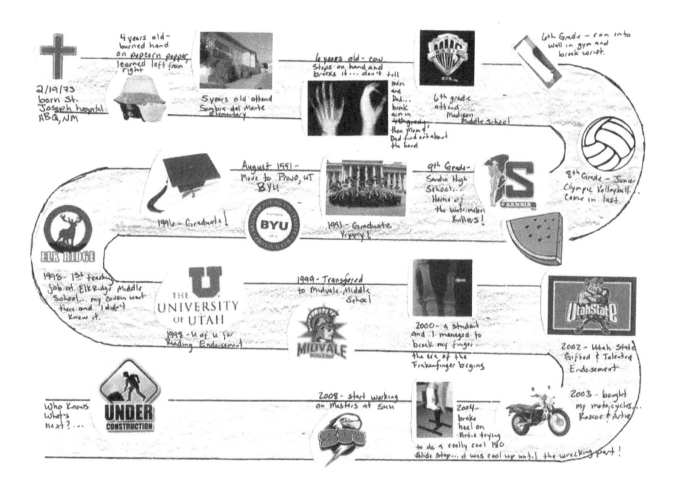

Pillar: Legacy

REFLECTION OF MY LIFE WORKSHEET

INSTRUCTIONS: Once they have completed their Life Map activity, complete the 'Reflection of My Life' questions.

1. Exchange your life-map with another participant in your group or with your mentor, after reviewing their life-map share how you feel about the person whose life-map you have reviewed.

   _____
   _____
   _____

2. What values do you notice reflected in the important events?

   _____
   _____
   _____
   _____

3. What would you change about your life-map if you could? Why?

   _____
   _____
   _____
   _____

4. Where are you going in the future?

   _____
   _____
   _____
   _____

5. List and describe 3 things you can do in your life stage now to make future life stages happen the way you'd like them to.

   _____
   _____
   _____

JOURNAL PAGES

Pillar: Legacy

Week 45 & 46 Activities

YOUTH ACTIVITIES

Pillar: Legacy

Creating a Legacy

LESSON VOCABULARY WORDS

INSTRUCTIONS: Study the vocabulary words listed below for a good understanding of each one.

1. **Acceptance**: the action or process of being received as adequate or suitable, typically to be admitted into a group.

2. **Gratitude:** the quality of being thankful; readiness to show appreciation for and to return kindness.

3. **Legacy Letter**: a written document of your values, experiences, and hard-earned life lessons.

COLLECTING LEGACY STORIES

Ask the following interview questions and record the answers on your cell phone:

a. Where did you grow up?
b. What were your parents like? Your siblings?
c. What do you remember about your grandparents?
d. Who were your friends?
e. What was school like for you?
f. What did you do for fun when you were a child? when you were a teenager?
g. What movies and songs did you like when you were young?
h. How did you meet your spouse?
i. What important lessons have you learned in your life?

Encourage your loved ones to tell the whole story about their life and the lives of their ancestors. Ask for the facts, dates, heirlooms, photographs, dates, etc. This doesn't have to be a big event. Make it a common occurrence around the dinner table, in the car, or at bedtime. Be respectful of their time and schedule a time to show them the video clip and discuss the video afterwards. Select your favorite story to share during your group discussion or your one-on-one time with your mentor.

CREATE A FAMILY TREE

From the video recordings and the conversations, create a family tree to track the family members you have talked to and those you have heard stories about. Do your research! Google the members to find additional information about your family members that wasn't shared on the Genealogy videos. You will be able to easily keep track of the family members and their placement on the family tree.

My Family Tree

JOURNAL PAGES

Legacy

"You get to decide the LEGACY that you leave." ~ www.WordsOnImages.com

Pillar: Legacy

EMPLOYEE OR COMMUNITY CITIZEN ACTIVITIES

Pillar: Legacy

Creating a Legacy

LESSON VOCABULARY WORDS

INSTRUCTIONS: Study the vocabulary words listed below for a good understanding of each one.

1. **Acceptance**: the action or process of being received as adequate or suitable, typically to be admitted into a group.

2. **Gratitude:** the quality of being thankful; readiness to show appreciation for and to return kindness.

3. **Legacy Letter**: a written document of your values, experiences, and hard-earned life lessons.

5 STEPS TO WRITE YOUR LEGACY LETTER

A 15-Minute Activity using the following 5 Steps to Write Your Legacy Letter instructions.

a. **Who is this letter for**: Could be addressed to family in general, or a specific friend or relative.

b. **Thank you**: Write what you appreciate, what you're grateful for about this person(s).

c. **3 things life taught me**: Next list your life lessons. (You might just list one initially and later add others.)

d. **What matters most – your values**: Say what's really important to you. Start with at least one of your values and add more later.

e. **In closing…**: Finally, end your letter and sign off, possibly adding a special saying or poem you like.

Process/Instructions:

a. Use a letter format.

   1. Be clear on your context. Provide a snapshot of the times and circumstances surrounding the event
   2. Tell your story. Be open and honest in your writings.
   3. Learned wisdom. What wisdom have you gleaned for the experiences you are sharing.
   4. The closer. A blessing that flows from your story and learning to the interested recipients of your letter.

b. Time Yourself and write for 15 minutes and no more.

c. Present the letter to the individual to honor them for their impact on your life.

(https://sixtyandme.com/write-legacy-letter/)

REFLECTIONS: After writing your legacy letter, write your reflections about your experience. Write for no more than 5-7 minutes. Keep your reflections with a copy of your letter in your personal legacy file. Be prepared to share your experience and what you learned overall from the experience.

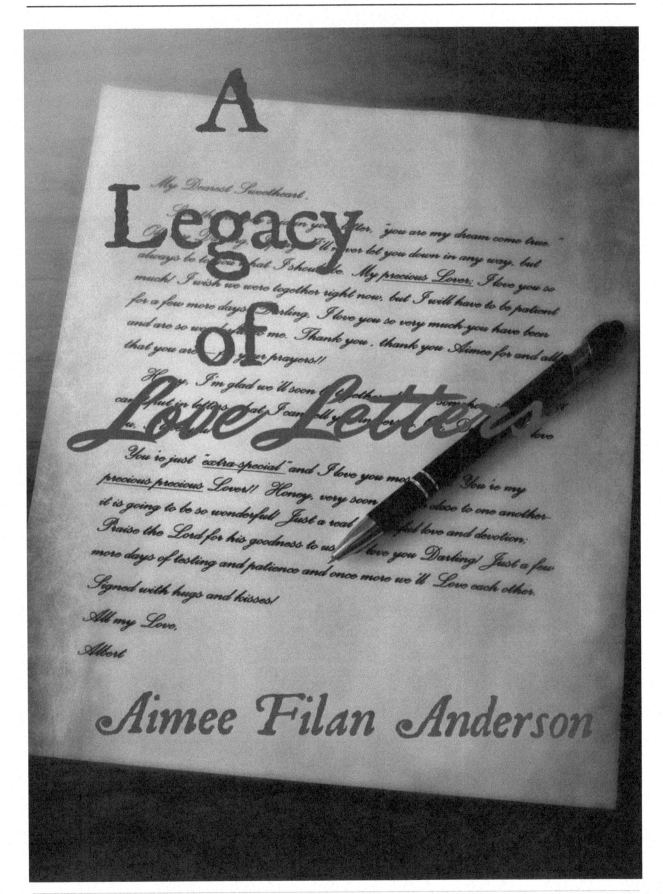

JOURNAL PAGES

Pillar: Legacy

Week 47 & 48 Activities

YOUTH ACTIVITIES

Pillar: Legacy

A Living Legacy

LESSON VOCABULARY WORDS

INSTRUCTIONS: Study the vocabulary words listed below for a good understanding of each one.

1. **Heroism:** someone who shows great courage and valor through their words and/or actions.

2. **Characteristics:** a special quality or trait that makes a person, thing, or group different from others.

3. **Social Responsibility**: involves an individual who is accountable for fulfilling their civic duty and that benefits the whole of society.

MY PERSONAL HERO ACTIVITY

What are personal heroes? Personal heroes are people who, in the opinion of others, has special achievements, abilities, or personal qualities and is regarded as a role model. A true hero is someone who does something heroic for the benefit of others. Their deed, act, performance, or accomplishment is not for their benefit alone.

Activity: Make a list of your personal heroes. Your list should contain family members, celebrities, athletes, etc. People who display values and behaviors you want to emulate. Your list cannot be based upon the amount of money the person has but based on who they are as a person. (i.e., if they select a basketball/football/soccer/tennis player, who are they off the court/field, when they are on the court do they display great sportsmanship.)

Discussion Questions:

1. Is it hard for you to say you are sorry or to be the bigger person? Why or Why not?

   _____
   _____
   _____

2. What did you learn being a hero and living legacy?

   _____
   _____
   _____

HERO DIAGRAM ACTIVITY:

Complete the *Hero Diagram Form* provided with this lesson plan. Once the form is completed, participate in a group discussion on who's a hero and living legacy.

Hero Video Activity: After watching the video, identify the hero in the story, and write down five things he/she did that identified him/her as a hero. Be prepared to share your list of characteristics from the video clip during the discussion time.

Characteristics of a hero

1. Bravery
2. Conviction
3. Courage
4. Determination
5. Helpful
6. Honesty
7. Inspirational
8. Moral integrity
9. Protective
10. Self-sacrifice
11. Selflessness
12. Strength

(https://www.verywellmind.com/characteristics-of-heroism-2795943#toc-12-characteristics-of-heroism)

REFLECTION: people who engage in acts of heroism have concern and care for the people around them, have a desire to inspire, empower and enable them to step up for what they believe in and be the hero in their own story.

Pillar: Legacy

CHARACTERISTICS OF A HERO

Intentional Mentoring Mentee's Workbook

HERO DIAGRAM WORKSHEET

For sections #1-5, write evidence or ideas that describe a hero from the video clip.

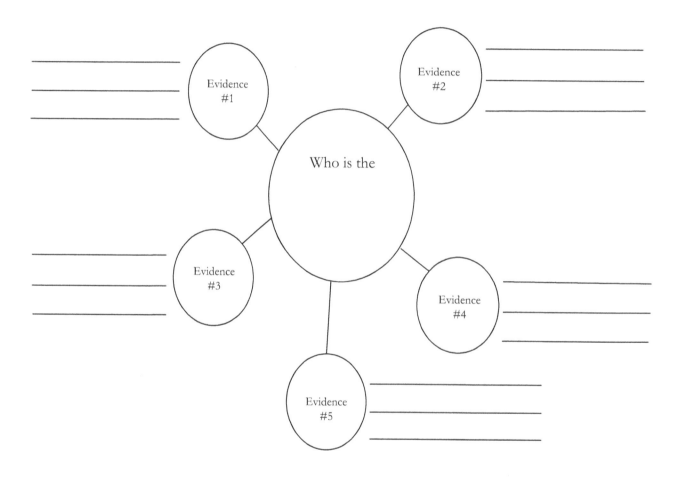

346 | P a g e

JOURNAL PAGES

Pillar: Legacy

EMPLOYEE OR COMMUNITY CITIZEN ACTIVITIES

Pillar: Legacy

A LIVING LEGACY

LESSON VOCABULARY WORDS

INSTRUCTIONS: Study the vocabulary words listed below for a good understanding of each one.

1. **Heroism:** someone who shows great courage and valor through their words and/or actions.
2. **Characteristics:** a special quality or trait that makes a person, thing, or group different from others.
3. **Social Responsibility:** involves an individual who is accountable for fulfilling their civic duty and that benefits the whole of society

REFLECTION: Living a legacy means putting a stamp on the future and contributing to future generations. People want to leave a legacy because they want to feel like their life mattered. Legacy is more about sharing what you have learned, not just what you have earned, and bequeathing values over valuables, as material wealth is only a small fraction of your legacy. A more holistic definition of legacy is when you are genuinely grounded in offering yourself and making a meaningful, lasting, and energizing contribution to humanity by serving a cause greater than your own. The requirements of a legacy are that you embrace your uniqueness, passionately immersing your whole self into life so that your gift will be to all and that you take responsibility to ensure that it will have a life beyond that of you, its creator, outliving and outlasting your time on earth.

Activity: To create a relationship with the future and live into it before it appears, choose one of the following activities and create a plan of action on how you will complete it:

a. Become committed to writing down your thoughts and memories daily in a Journal.
b. Create a recipe journal with family stories attached to each recipe.
c. Research and select a cause or non-profit that supports your family's beliefs. Donate your time and finances as a means of support. Keep pictures and videos of your interactions with the cause or non-profit to share with your family and friends.
d. Create a plan to plant a tree to honor the birth of each child born in the family, on family land or in a park, your family visits often.
e. Plan a family gathering to honor your family's elders and set aside time for them to share their hopes, dreams, and wisdom with the family. Record it and make copies for each family to have one.

Discussion Questions:

1. How can you put your stamp on the future?

2. What is unique about you? What talent, skill or ability do you have that can be used to live the legacy you desire to leave?

3. After watching the video clip, share how he told Akeelah to show up?

4. Why do you think he told her that bit of advice?

5. What are your goals and/or aspirations?

REFLECTION: *"Your story is the greatest legacy that you will leave to your friends, family and loved ones. It's the longest lasting legacy you will leave to your heirs."* – Steve Saint

Pillar: Legacy

what is my legacy?

LEGACY #1:

WHAT AM I DOING TO CULTIVATE & GROW HEALTHY ROOTS IN THIS AREA?

LEGACY #2

LEGACY #3

kristagilbert.com

Intentional Mentoring Mentee's Workbook

What will your legacy be? Fill these steppingstones with things you want people to remember about you.

Build your legacy!

Leave a Legacy...

www.teacherspayteachers.com

JOURNAL PAGES

Pillar: Legacy

"no legacy is so rich as honesty."

WILLIAM SHAKESPEARE

BIBLIOGRAPHY

1. *5 Ways to Teach Kids to Live Life Well*, www.Sunshine-Parenting.com
2. *Health Benefits of Social Interactions*, www.mercycare.org
3. *Self-Love and What it Means*, www.bbrfoundation.org, February 12, 2020
4. *A Seven Step Prescription for Self-love* Article, www.psychologytoday.com, by Deborah Khoshaba, PsyD., 3/27/2012
5. *HW Action Plan Template*, https://www.healthierwork.act.gov.au/wp-content/uploads/2015/01/HW_Action_Plan_template.pdf
6. *4 Better Ways to Respond to how are you that I'm Good*, https://www.sigconsult.com/blog/2019/02/4-better-ways-to-respond-to-how-are-you-than-im-good?source=google.com
7. *What is Workplace Bullying*, https://www.healthline.com/health/workplace-bullying#What-is-workplace-bullying?
8. *John Maxwell on Leadership*, https://www.td.org/magazines/td-magazine/john-maxwell-on-leadership, by ATD Staff, February 8, 2013
9. *Develop Leadership Skills with a Mentor*, https://www.togetherplatform.com/blog/mentoring-develop-leadership-skills-with-a-mentor, by Matthew Reeves, August 1, 2021
10. *4 Essential Traits of a Mentor Leader*, https://www.allprodad.com/4-essential-traits-of-a-mentor-leader/
11. *Develop Leadership Skills by Mentoring*, https://www.reliableplant.com/Read/29332/mentoring-develops-leadership, by Debbie Zmorenski, from excerpt by Bozeman, Feeney, 2007,)
12. *6 Reasons Why Servant Leadership is Best*, https://www.rootinc.com/why-servant-leadership-really-works/, by Jim Haudan, October 26, 2020
13. *Servant Leader as Change Agents - A Lean Journey*, by Tim McMahon, April 11, 2022, http://www.aleanjourney.com/2022/04/servant-leader-as-change-agents.html)
14. *How to Make a Budget*, https://www.tiaa.org/public/learn/personal-finance-101/how-to-make-a-budget
15. *Expense Tracker*, www.ShiningMom.com
16. *Character Trait Crafts Activities for Kids*, https://www.craftionary.net/character-trait-crafts-activities-kids/
17. Creating A Life Map, https://www.iroquoiscsd.org/cms/lib/NY19000365/Centricity/Domain/79/Creating-a-life-map.ppt
18. *How to Create a Life Map with Examples*, https://www.edrawmind.com/how-to-create-a-life-map-with-examples.html)

19. *Characteristics of Heroism*, (https://www.verywellmind.com/characteristics-of-heroism-2795943#toc-12-characteristics-of-heroism)

20. *29 Questions to ask your Mentor in your next Meeting*, https://www.togetherplatform.com/blog/29-questions-to-ask-your-mentor-in-your-next-meeting

21. *Therapist Aid Worksheet*, www.TherapistAid.com

22. https://www.pinterest.com/pin/2603712269545288/

23. *You get to decide the LEGACY that you leave* Quote, www.WordsOnImages.com

24. *Worksheets and Templates*, www.teacherspayteachers.com

25. *What is my legacy Worksheet*, www.Kristagilbert.com

ABOUT THE AUTHOR

Dr. Kenneth D. Davis, Ed.D.

Dr. Kenneth D. Davis recently retired from the Houston Independent School District as their Executive Director of Equity and Outreach. Prior to this role, he was the Area Superintendent of the South Region, Assistant Superintendent of Equity and Outreach, Principal at Jack Yates High School, School Support Officer (principal supervisor), and Principal at Dowling (now Lawson) Middle School. He has had many titles and positions in the past 31 years, which began in the classroom molding and educating young minds.

Dr. Davis has a lengthy and successful track record in the business of education. Starting from the classroom he rose from classroom teacher to being selected as the campus teacher of the year, but the accolades were far from over. Dr. Davis became an assistant principal after his assistant superintendent noticed his flare and magic with teaching and 'encouraged' him to pursue a master's degree in educational administration. In doing so, he learned the role well and became a principal in the Lamar Consolidated Independent Schools within four years.

In the Lamar Consolidated Independent Schools, Dr. Davis moved the school from low performing to an Exemplary status with the support of an open-minded and hardworking staff. After two consecutive years, Dr. Davis was assigned to open a new elementary campus, McNeill, and that school also experienced Exemplary Campus performance. Dr. Davis had been nominated and selected as the Houston Area Alliance of Black School Educator's Teacher of the year, Principal of the Year twice) and awarded the National Distinguished Principal (NDP) for Texas Award, the highest honor an educator can receive.

Dr. Davis continues to share his knowledge and experience in supporting students by creating and developing districtwide mentoring programs like the Ascending To Men (ATM) and Resilient Outstanding Sisters Exemplifying Success (ROSES) that support students in need of mentorship as they matriculate through the educational system successfully and on to a career, college, and/or the military. He continues to be a positive and supportive force in education.

Dr. Davis credits his long-lasting career in education to building relationships, honoring education for all students, growing and developing teachers, and working to build strong instructional and visionary leaders. He works countless hours teaching at the University of Houston to guide instructional leaders to build reading skills for students that struggle and teaching the Equity in The Classroom course. Dr. Davis speaks and presents to future leaders across the country and has worked with several organizations to build and support future administrators through Columbia University and Birmingham City Schools. He mentors current principals, deans, assistant principals, instructional specialists, and teachers.